The Art of Free Travel

Patrick Jones is an artist, poet, permaculturist, essayist and blogger. His favourite bush tucker is hand-speared coal-cooked fish.

Meg Ulman is an artist, community gardener, fermenter, blogger, and writer. Meg's favourite bush tucker is the burdekin plum.

The Art of Free Travel

A frugal family adventure

Patrick Jones and Meg Ulman

NEWSOUTH

A NewSouth book
Published by
NewSouth Publishing
University of New South Wales Press Ltd
University of New South Wales
Sydney NSW 2052
AUSTRALIA
newsouthpublishing.com

© Patrick Jones & Meg Ulman 2015
First published 2015

10 9 8 7 6 5 4 3 2 1

This book is copyright. Apart from any fair dealing for the purpose of private study, research, criticism or review, as permitted under the *Copyright Act*, no part of this book may be reproduced by any process without written permission. Inquiries should be addressed to the publisher.

National Library of Australia
Cataloguing-in-Publication entry
Creator: Jones, Patrick, 1970–, author.
Title: The art of free travel: a frugal family adventure
ISBN: 9781742234434 (paperback)
　　　9781742242125 (ebook)
　　　9781742247458 (epdf)
Subjects: Jones, Patrick, 1970—Travel—Australia
Ulman, Meg—Travel—Australia
Bicycle touring—Australia—Anecdotes.
Bicycle touring—Economic aspects—Australia.
Travel writing—Australia.
Australia—Description and travel.
Other Creators/Contributors:Ulman, Meg, author.
Number: 796.640994

Design Josephine Pajor-Markus
Cover design Xou Digital
Cover images Front: Jay Town / Newspix Back: Artist as family
Illustrations Patrick Jones
Printer Griffin Printing

All reasonable efforts were taken to obtain permission to use copyright material reproduced in this book, but in some cases copyright could not be traced. The authors welcome information in this regard.

This book is printed on paper using fibre supplied from plantation or sustainably managed forests.

*For our dear friends Peter O'Mara and Brett Adamson —
tireless workers for justness*

Contents

Prologue 1
Becoming car-free 2
Planting the seed 16
Preparations 29
On the road 47
Law-breakers 71
Embracing uncertainty 101
Camp Liberty 119
Becoming north 139
Palm Island 161
Opening out 179
Hope Vale 198
Heading home 217
What we took when we left home 239
Our list of free food and medicine 243
Related reading 252
We couldn't have done it without you 255

Prologue

— Meg —

I finally agreed to travelling around Australia for a year as a family one night in bed. The boys Zephyr and Woody were asleep in their room, our dog Zero snuggled up with one of them. Patrick and I had been quietly reading and just after we turned off our bedside lights, we leaned towards each other and kissed. It wasn't a particularly stirring kiss; tired from another long day we pulled away and lay there in the dark, feeling the other's breath and sensing the outline of each other's bodies as our eyes grew accustomed to the dark.

And it was then at that moment that I knew. This man, whom I had known and loved for seven years, was my man and I trusted him. I had laughed at the absurdity of his saying 'I love you' the first night we had kissed, but had later praised him for his foresight.

We had made a life together in seven years; a big, wondrous, full, uncomplicated life.

It was time for a little danger.

'I'm in,' I whispered.

Becoming car-free

– Patrick –

'I want to get rid of one of the cars,' I announced one day to my then partner Mel. 'I'll walk through the Wombat to the shop each day; it will only take an hour or so.'

I had done some basic maths and with petrol, servicing, registration, insurance and depreciation, each of our cars was costing us nearly $10,000 a year. But there wasn't much interest in the idea across the room.

'We could actually draw a nominal wage from the shop if I walked to work,' I continued. 'And I wouldn't have to keep taking on building work to subsidise it.'

At that time ten years ago I was working long hours and suffering from anxiety, sometimes so severe that I would walk round and round reeling off all the things I felt caged by in my life until I became a panicked coil of limbs and exasperation.

That day, I was arguing the economic logic of doing away with a car, but there was much more to it. I wanted to walk through the Wombat Forest to my beloved bookshop because I knew it would be good for my wellbeing.

'It would be really impractical,' Mel argued. 'What about the dark and cold of the winter months?'

She had a point. We lived in Lyonville, a cool-highland, one-pub, no-shop town situated on the tailbone of the Great Dividing Range in Central Victoria. The bookshop was in the larger town of Trentham that boasted a population of 660 people then, and like Lyonville gets snowfalls every winter and is famous for its black frosts that shatter tree limbs.

But I needed more simplicity. It was a 14-kilometre round trip on foot, and even if impracticality was my intuitive response then, I wanted to trust in it.

Living in rural Victoria made me so car-dependent: to get milk, meet a friend, go to work, attend a meeting. I was too often cooped up in a metal bubble on four wheels, technologically brilliant but ecologically stupid. I resented flashing past environments rich in intricate life but could only be experienced and better understood by going slow. I didn't want conditioned air, I didn't want radio heads, I didn't want speed and glass and oil wars.

I wanted relationships. I wanted intimacy and connection to the places I was moving through. I wanted dirt and scat and moss and mushroom to ignite my senses, as much as people and their technologies.

I was a keen walker, though my long walks alone in the Wombat had begun to dry up. Life as a new father had become busier, with much less sleep. I still relished my time in the bush, which flowed on from our southern boundary for thousands of hectares, taking newborn Zephyr into the damp forest sedgelands that were older than the dinosaurs. But these shorter father-and-child walks were not the heavy doses of alone time I needed. What I found most frustrating was knowing that the simple act of walking relieved my anxiety.

For one reason or another my plans to be carless would have to wait for another five years, through Mel's and my breakup, a turbulent though exciting readjustment period, then the blossoming of a new relationship.

After about a year of singledom, a move to nearby Daylesford and, with a switch of just one consonant from Mel to Meg, my life transformed significantly.

My new partner Meg rode a bicycle, took what little public transport came and went from the small hilly town we both lived in, and she rented a house close to the local shops and services, which meant she rarely used her car. I was attracted to Meg for so many reasons. Watching the film *Fargo* with her in a room full of people one night, I listened to her quiet sighs of compassion as she engaged with certain characters. On hearing her empathy I knew we could have a future. I also knew I wanted to be with Meg because of her environmental ethics.

When I was arguing with Mel about getting rid of one of our cars, I was also obsessing about the problems of the society I was born into. I saw money as a form of social control and sensed how this control leads to lifestyles that are anything but altruistic.

When Zephyr came into our little community I was already quite active in the Wombat Forest Society, recording the damage to riparian zones in logging coupes, taking water samples and photographs to use as evidence of breaches committed by the woodchip industry. I could see how environments such as the Wombat were increasingly exploited to grow the state's and the nation's economies, as if no other socioeconomic reality was possible.

I was also making environmental artworks in this forest. Once I planted an extensive copse of mixed eucalypt saplings into a mountainous pile of prostrate logs; a pile that was to be chipped and shipped to Japan to be pulped for hamburger wrappers. With a hand-driven auger and a two-inch drill bit I bored 60 holes at various intervals into messmates, peppermints and swamp gums and carefully planted into the holes the young saplings. The logs weren't collected for several months and over this time the saplings began to grow, feeding from the moisture of the green wood and my occasional watering.

One day the pile was not there anymore. I wasn't hopeful of resurrection, but rather performing a private ritual of loss and ecological renewal. My audience for this work wasn't the typical art crowd, but the diesel-scented men who collected the logs for a wage.

I was thirty-five and getting into my mid-life crisis fairly early. The five-year-old bookshop ended with the twelve-year relationship, and I found myself taking on more and more building work, which inevitably required me to keep driving a vehicle. I had built the little home that Zeph was born in and had learned enough skills doing so to hire myself out. While I enjoyed the physicality and the mental challenges of building work, it was not what I really wanted to be doing. It was exhausting, especially having to deal with the constantly changing desires of clients. On top of this I didn't have, or want to get, a builder's ticket or an architecture degree. I had two fairly disposable arts degrees already, a whopping Higher Education Contribution Scheme debt, and I had no interest in joining what I saw as the limitations of a scholarly life in the city – too much theory, not enough practice; too much bureaucracy, not enough humus.

So I designed and built small houses and studios for owner–builders and others who were happy to bend some of the state's building regulations. It seemed inevitable that the longer I stayed in the game the time would come that I'd have to get certified. Building for me was a means to an end, not a life's practice or direction. At the peak of my building career I'd designed and built a beautiful home for a couple who, after I had spent a year pouring all my blood, sweat and tears into, boasted at their housewarming that they'd designed it. Yes, their names were on the paperwork as the owner–designers for legal reasons, but their signatures on the page were the extent of their creativity. They had sucked all the life out of me on that project. I lost money building their precious home, which they sold a year later for

Becoming car-free

four times what it cost them (and me) to build. I vowed never to line the pockets of such people again.

All I really wanted to do was carry on my practice as a poet of ecology and a critic of society, which translates in Aussie to being a wanker. The eco-poet–critic job doesn't really wash well with many people; it's not like I'm a teacher or an accountant.

My self-fashioned vocation as a permanent student of ecology was to better understand how humans could rebuild ecological societies such as those that existed in Australia before 1788. I rather romantically saw my bookshop as an intellectual hub where I could converse and debate, host readings, write in the quiet times and drink too much coffee. Fellow writer Peter Timms and eco-poet Michael Farrell were among those who came and read. The bookshop became my own decentralised micro-university.

The bookshop was also an unofficial drop-in centre for the bereft and lonely, and on one occasion I found myself entering the garage of one of my regulars as he was about to hang himself. I'd trusted my intuition to call around after he'd come in for his morning coffee and behaved atypically. He said later that he'd thought nobody cared about him. The other thing that kept him in the land of the living was learning; an avid reader, he always came along to our guest readings and lectures, and asked great questions.

Eventually I recognised that to become a fully fledged wanker I needed to earn less, not more, and in order to live with less money I needed to become car-free. I was working for about a quarter of every year just to pay for the wear and tear on my tools and to keep my vehicle on the road. I no longer wanted to be a victim of such an economic ideology, especially one that normalised pollution. And although I didn't know it at the time, all this thinking about environmental damage and economic entrapment was going to lead to a really big, freedom-seeking adventure with a gutsy lover, two bonza sons and a garrulous Jack Russell.

When Meg and I first got together we each had separate cars, bank accounts and rental homes, but all that changed fairly quickly. After about a year together we found some land in Daylesford, moved on to it a small, fold-up house that came on the back of a truck, and soon started merging everything except our libraries, which we kept on independent bookshelves. Meg's, an exciting ramshackle of world novels, magazines and non-fiction; mine, a meticulously ordered, slightly pompous collection of environmental, societal and experimental literatures. I finally cleared my credit-card debts and, like Meg, opened a single debit-card account. We had what we had, and nothing more.

One of the first times Meg and I hooked up in Melbourne, my friend Jason Workman and I had just finished a day performing the street-art practice we called free-dragging. Free-dragging is a kind of physical graffiti where our bodies act as the spray paint, marking the metropolis, making marks that quickly became physically untraceable but are etched into the retinas of passers-by.

This involved dressing in drag or in business suits and jumping around the city, scaling trees and buildings, rolling around or sleeping in the street, swinging off signs and tram shelters, perching on things like we were birds of prey and generally creating a mutant form of parkour or free-running. This unsanctioned anti-art in the traditions of the Aussie ratbag and the International Situationists, which was filmed by surveilling friends, saw us invited to America by a non-profit arts organisation in Richmond, Virginia. Meg met us in a bar afterwards. Jason and I were both still dressed in skirts, stockings, hairclips and a veneer of the city's toxic dust as our face powder. This will either make or break us, I thought, as she walked up to greet me.

Meg fell in love with a man in women's clothes sitting confidently crossed-legged in a bar full of suits. I fell in love with a woman who pulled up an image on her phone to show me her drag-king persona Spiro Lina, the motor mechanic.

'Snap!' she shouted.

It was on. And later on – on top and under – we sank and drew and pushed and gripped and climbed and tossed and threw and bit and sucked each other into coupledom.

After turning down the generously funded trip to America on environmental grounds, I started to read more seriously about permaculture and other forms of applied and social ecology. Permaculture is an Australian concept gone global that aims to design human settlements that produce no waste, where food, fodder, fuel, fibre, medicine and building materials all come from one's own bioregion, and are produced or recycled to mitigate environmental damage and social injustice.

Meg and I seemed capable of influencing each other in our most positive interests. We couldn't wait to start our own food garden, but it would take some time before we were ready to have a child together. There were certainly things that were difficult in those early days, mainly involving my desperation to share half of the parenting of four-year-old Zephyr. But I was now in a relationship where I felt my interests and desires were being heard and Meg, to my great delight, had not only taken on Zeph as a stepson, but Mel as an ex-wife. This resulted in greater trust between the two houses, and then the reestablishment of a friendship with Mel, who is now Woody's goddest-of-the-gods mother, or whatever the non-monotheistic version of that role is called.

The first car had been relatively easy to give up, although Meg struggled initially with the idea of composting our second. The car had belonged to her grandmother, so there was a fair bit of sentimentalism on her part. But once we'd made up our minds, or rather, once Meg agreed, we parked the car in the carport and tried not to drive it for an entire year. We bought Zeph a bike and one for me, and together with Meg on hers we started

Becoming car-free

using our treadlies as our primary mode of travel.

Not long after I brought home my retrofitted tip bike that had been hotted up by our handy and creative friend Josh, I had to get to a meeting in a nearby town about 15 kilometres away. I decided to ride. It was the furthest distance I would have ridden in about twenty years and I left myself two hours to get there as I had no idea how long it would take. I was fairly cocky when I left home, strapping my helmet over a woollen beanie because it was so cold. After a few hours, when Meg still hadn't received a message that I'd arrived safely, she phoned to make sure I was OK. Exhausted and freezing after the one-kilometre uphill ride to town, I'd called a friend who was also going to the meeting to ask if he could pick me up from the café where I was waiting by the open fire, drinking tea.

'Epic fail, Dad,' was eight-year-old Zeph's greeting when I returned home that evening.

Slowly and without realising it we all increased our bike fitness so that when we were ready to sell our second car we couldn't believe we had ever needed it to zip up to town to the post office or the library, or down to the food co-op in nearby Hepburn Springs 4 kilometres away. During that year we biked and walked everywhere and developed a hardiness to the weather. We didn't get sick over the entire winter, a first for our household. We bought warm socks from the local woollen mill, op-shop gloves and warmer jackets and carried our pocket umbrellas with us everywhere.

Once in the pouring rain a car slowed down beside us as we were walking home from town. We politely declined a lift from our friend who was driving.

'I feel so terrible that you guys are walking and I'm nice and cosy in my car,' she called out through the open window.

But we were not in need of sympathy. It was invigorating living like this, as freeing as it was pleasurable. Sometimes Meg and I would walk home in the dark from a night out and afterwards confide to one another that the walk there and back had been the highlight of the evening. Walking, says the American writer Rebecca Solnit, is the ideal pace for thinking and, I would add, for conversing and working through life's enigmas.

Although we loved our newfound fitness and hardiness, we still occasionally drove. And each time we did, we wrote down in a logbook the distance we had driven and the purpose of the journey. Mel, who needed to regularly come into town anyway, was happy to drop off and pick up Zeph at changeover times. The majority of the trips we made were under 5 kilometres – collecting horse manure, grabbing that last-minute ingredient or bottle of wine, or when we were running late for something – except for the drive out to Zephyr's school in Yandoit, 22 kilometres away. We carpooled for the half-week Zeph was now with us with two other families, who very generously offered to take him to school and bring him home if we did end up going completely car-free. While a generous offer, we declined, and with

Becoming car-free

Mel's agreement we enrolled Zeph in a small community school the following year that was just around the corner from our home. We saw the remainder of the school year out at Yandoit Primary and were one step closer to selling the car.

It might be chilly for much of the year in Daylesford, but the summer months are prone to bushfires. We are surrounded by thousands of acres of gums trees, therefore millions of litres of highly flammable eucalyptus oil. During each fire season the boot of the car was often home to hard drives and legal documents, photos and other keepsakes, which Meg arranged. I had spent most of my life in the country and was more confident about what to do in a fire than my city-raised girlfriend. Since we've been together we've had to evacuate our house on a few occasions because of approaching bushfires and each time the circumstances were different.

But we felt all these challenges could be met, that they were not going to stop us from being car-free in the country. If we needed to get to the hospital with a broken bone or a chainsaw cut through the knee (which had happened to me a few years earlier), there was a cab around the corner, or a mate at the end of the phone. We would carpool with friends to parties out of town, give them petrol money or garden produce and reduce their carbon footprints by filling up their seats.

Just as it was with free-dragging, chance played a greater role in our lives when we were without a car.

Sometimes we'd have to go to a nearby town, catch the morning bus over and have several hours to wait until the evening bus returned. In this time we would explore and wander, catch up with a friend, read or while away the day, seeing where chance and our thoughts would take us. Without the running costs and so-called convenience of our cars we found we had more time to muse and be, well, free. All of this was priming us, preparing us. But for what?

If I had known in advance all the arguments, thinking and planning that would go into becoming carless, I may never have dared to act. Within our economic system it's easy to get trapped in a cycle of consumption. Banks take our worked-for coin and gleefully profit by turning our earnings into ever-expanding debt. Mel and I had been wholly dependent on our cars to make the money that would service our way of life. We were in an unstoppable cycle of debt-making and debt-servicing.

But however unlikely it had seemed initially, several years later it happened. Finally, we were ready.

That morning Meg and I walked through town and up to the very social Sunday market to meet Mel and Zeph, mentioning to several people that we wanted to sell our car. By the time we'd arrived home there was a message on our answering machine from a man we didn't know telling us he'd like to buy it.

There was no going back. We were finally car-free

– and a little bit closer to discovering the very possible art of free travel.

Planting the seed

– Meg –

'But Woody is sleeping through the night now!' I explained. It wasn't an excuse, a reason or even an argument. It was a simple truth, if such a thing exists. It was cold outside, a clear June night, and we were in bed early, eager for the cosiness of our flannelette sheets, which we had just put on for the first time that winter.

'Just think about it,' Patrick said, sitting at the end of the bed, rubbing my feet to warm them.

'I don't need to.'

'Meg ...'

'My parents have just moved to town.'

'They'll still be here when we get back.'

'How will we afford it?'

'We could rent the house.'

'What about the garden? The chooks, the ducks?'

'We'll make sure we get the right tenants. Or we could sell? Then we could travel for longer – maybe indefinitely?'

Planting the seed

Folk-rocker Billy Bragg's lyric about couples making important decisions in bed was true for us too. Although we didn't make a decision that night, like many couples, collecting our thoughts happened at the end of each day – after dinner, putting the kids to bed and household chores, after we'd flossed and brushed – and when we were finally horizontal.

'We are happy here!' I continued, touching the fingers on my left hand with every point I made. 'Our lives are fulfilling. We have great friends. The community gardens. Our band. We don't need to escape from anything.'

But the seed had been planted: a trip. A *big* trip.

It's not that Patrick is more persuasive or that my list of reasons to stay put was inconsequential. It was the right time in so many ways. But still I wasn't sure.

'What about Zeph? His mum might not agree.'

We were now home-educating Zeph – school was way too enclosed for our lively boy. We didn't have the issue of taking him out of school, but I just couldn't imagine Mel letting us take her only child away for a whole year.

'And what about our sourdough starter? Will we bake bread on the road? What will we do about nappies? I refuse to buy disposables. What about Zeida? [My 95-year-old grandfather.] What about your thesis? What happens if you need to do a massive rewrite?'

For the last four years Patrick had been working on

his doctorate. He was writing the final draft and was looking forward to sending it off and having a big ol' break. We all were. He was the one doing the actual writing, but it was a whole family affair. In fact several times I had imagined aloud that all of us, including Zero, would have to be fitted out in gowns and caps as surely we would all be graduating. Our names mightn't appear on the certificate, but in actuality it was ours: his thesis charted our family's transition from a high reliance on crude oil to a much reduced one, by replacing global resources with local ones, and increasingly going without. We had all been a part of it. And we all really needed a break.

As part of his research Patrick had written a paper to present at a symposium. The paper was about walked-for food, and focussed on how our ancestors traditionally obtained their livelihoods within a low-carbon economy. As part of the presentation, we decided to walk to the symposium in Melbourne, 130 kilometres away.

Ordinarily whenever we travel to Melbourne we take public transport: a walk, a bus and a train, which takes about two hours. But it seemed fitting, given Patrick's paper, that we walked this time. As a somewhat new car-free family we wanted to see how far we could push this very ancient mode of transport. A walk like this isn't a stroll in the park, but it isn't absurdly far either. We gave ourselves five days.

My apple cake was still in the oven when a small gathering of family and friends arrived to send us off. But the cake wasn't the only thing that wasn't ready. As

Planting the seed

our small house began filling up with people we were finalising what shoes we'd wear, how many cloth nappies we needed and how many kilos of oats to pack. We were still decanting honey from a bucket into a small jar, and needed to explain to our housesitter how to look after our sixteen chickens and three ducks, and we couldn't find the compass. We had considered taking a pram in which we'd push seven-month-old Woody but decided instead to put him in a baby carrier that Patrick and I would take turns wearing. We had to wear all 9 kilos of him on our front, as we each needed to carry a backpack with our tent, sleeping bags, clothes, rain jackets, nappies, food, water and other necessities such as a camera and first-aid kit.

If we had had all the time in the world it would have been so much simpler. But we didn't. We had to average 26 kilometres a day, carrying all our own gear and some food and water, bush-bashing through the Wombat Forest across the Great Dividing Range with only a compass. Only Patrick didn't realise the compass he found in Zeph's room, as we all rushed the last of the pack, was not the real thing.

We were sent off with hearty fanfare and great excitement. After an hour of light-hearted exuberance, walking around Lake Daylesford and through the town's southern streets to the forest's edge, we realised we were carrying way too much gear. Early the next morning, after a freezing night with little sleep, we packed up our sad, damp camp and walked with our aches and pains for several hours under low cloud in what we thought was the right direction. Patrick kept reading the compass, trying to work out the discrepancy between his intuition and what the instrument was telling us. The sun was completely absent to give us a bearing. What resulted was absolute confusion, then successive chapters of rage from the tallest and oldest member of our tribe.

Sometime after lunch, we realised that our romantic notions of a lovely, challenging but bonding, family experience were chafed and blistered, just as our bodies were. Patrick's mood became increasingly dark as he stormed off ahead, determined to chop his way through the dense understorey. We followed behind, walking slower because I wanted to protect the boys and me from Patrick's mood. Every time we laughed or sang he yelled at us for not taking the situation seriously, for mucking around instead of focussing on catching up to him. Being lost was a serious issue, but surely we all didn't have to be punished.

'What's his problem?' eleven-year-old Zeph complained. 'I could have told him the compass came from a Christmas cracker.'

After several hours, we realised we had walked in a giant circle when we crossed a dirt track we recognised. To say we were devastated implies we were aware of our emotions, but we were even too tired for that.

'Woody's so bloody heavy!' Patrick groaned into the forest. 'I can't carry him on my front, and my pack, as well as navigate. I just can't do bloody everything!'

Although it was true he was carrying the stress of

the situation for all of us while mentally preparing for the symposium, it was lil ol' me, 25 kilos lighter than him, who had mostly carried Woody, as well as my pack.

By mid-afternoon we had no idea where we were, but at least the clouds had cleared. Using our solar logic we eventually managed to find a major forest road heading in the direction of where Patrick guessed the small town of Blackwood to be. Pretty soon a ute drove past slowly enough to see our hitchhiking thumbs waving excitedly.

'Oh, hi there,' Patrick managed once they'd stopped.

With much relief and gratitude we all piled in. Woody and I crammed into the cab, while Zeph, Patrick and Zero hopped on the ute's tray laden with two shot foxes and a pile of firewood. Fifteen minutes later we arrived in Blackwood, 30 kilometres from home. We had been dreaming of plundering the shelves of the general store for treats but had arrived five minutes before closing time to find the doors shut and bolted. There was no other shop in town. We sat in silence on a nearby bench.

'I am so sorry,' Patrick said slowly. 'I didn't mean to take my stress out on you guys.'

But we weren't really ready for an apology. We were hurt and felt bashed and bruised all over. The whole ordeal had been punishing on all of us.

It was a beautiful, still afternoon now that we could appreciate it, although the sun was setting and it was starting to get cold. One by one we summoned the nerve to take off our shoes. We compared our sores and blisters, rubbing the little watery bubbles that lined our heels and toes. We sat there for a long time listing all the things we would do differently next time, wondering over and over how we could have been so damn silly not to have even tried on our packs before we left, or tested out the compass.

We weighed up our options and decided that Zephyr, Woody, Zero and I would go home, while Patrick would continue walking, with a lightened pack, alone. An hour later, Mel arrived in her car to take us home.

'This country is huge!' I laughed. 'We can't even make it to Melbourne and you want to travel the whole continent?'

Although we hadn't all successfully walked to Melbourne, and although I had felt embarrassed by my failure, our attempt had evoked something in us.

'Next time we try something like this,' we told each other once Patrick had returned from the symposium, 'let's practise, do the research, and ensure we have the right gear.'

But a year-long trip?

It still felt crazy to me, as did so many things that Patrick had suggested, even though they had elicited a positive life-changing about-face in the end.

It had been Patrick's idea to buy the land we live on. It was going cheap and I could see why. When he first took me to look at it I almost laughed in his face. The ground was completely uneven and boggy, and there

Planting the seed

was only one tree on the block that we weren't sure was ours or the neighbour's.

But I trusted. And it turned out that the clay-lined, quarter-acre ugly duckling was ideal for growing food on. It was a ten-minute walk to town and a three-minute walk into the forest. And the big beautiful oak tree on our north side, which we now seasonally harvest to make acorn meal, was ours. And the perfect height to hang a rope swing from.

It had also been Patrick's suggestion to have a child together.

But how will we manage a baby without a car? I wondered.

We have friends in various cities around the world who don't rely on cars to ferry their kids around, but in a small regional town without hourly buses, trains or trams, I couldn't see how it was possible. We had had dozens of conversations about having a child – I was in my mid-thirties – but there didn't seem to be any urgency. For a long time Patrick could flip a coin either way. He loved being a dad but had been traumatised by Zephyr's irregular sleeping habits.

Zeph has always loved babies and since he was very young had been begging us for a brother.

'Are you two sexing yet?' he'd often ask.

I was happy not to have a child of my own – did the world really need another human? – and anyway, I had Zephyr in my life and three nieces nearby, so I was satisfied. The decision was one I might lament, but I was happy to make room for the regret.

'Think of all the time I'll have to myself to drink tea and read books on the couch, or to have a quiet thought without interruption!' I joked.

But the suggestion that we bring a new little person into the world was an idea whose time had arrived, and we all knew it.

But a baby seemed bigger than avoiding buying anything in plastic, becoming a paperless household (no mean feat for a family of writers), and relying on public transport despite all the waiting. A baby was more than boycotting supermarkets and air travel.

Then there was the small matter of a vasectomy to be reversed and a string of miscarriages to contend with. But after these hurdles and an easy pregnancy, there was the joy and fatigue and wonder of everyday life with a baby.

We first took Woody camping when he was four months old. Together with three other families, two of whom also had newborns, we spent a relaxing week swimming and playing at the beach. We had taken public transport, and had carried all our own gear. But unlike our trek towards Melbourne, we didn't have to carry our own food and water. It was a great holiday, though it had been so nice to return to our own beds and produce garden and showers and washing machine. And, if we're being completely honest, our toaster too. Is there anything that compares to the domestic delight of sitting down to a pot of tea and a plate of toast?

'But Woody is sleeping through the night now!' I said again. I had visions of all our hard work being undone, of Woody being unsettled in the tent each night and my being exhausted all the time, too tired to enjoy the country and people we encountered on this year-long trip. And camping. Every. Single. Night.

Don't get me wrong, I love camping. We often went on camping holidays when I was growing up. We lived in suburban Melbourne but our block of land was just over an acre. Down the back, my sisters and I would spend hours playing, digging and building under the huge walnut tree, where I felt there was truly space for me to express my tomboy tendencies. We had a holiday house in Deloraine, Tasmania, 100 kilometres from Cradle Mountain. Because we weren't permanently there, its mudbrick walls would fill with spiders, mice and bats. One night, after I had turned off the light from my top bunk using a plank of wood, the air came alive with furry microbats. Responding to my sister Kate's and my screams, Mum came in with a butterfly net she used to catch the bats, before releasing them into the night.

Decades later when I told Zeph this story, he asked why my father hadn't come into our room. Until then it had never occurred to me that fathers were traditionally the ones to rescue their daughters. In our house, although Dad was practical, he was a doctor, and spent most of his time at home working in his office. It was Mum who engaged in more earthly endeavours. She looked after our garden, our compost, and the day-to-day triumph and drama of raising four daughters. Mum never wore make-up and rarely made me brush my hair.

On bushwalks, she loved to point out trees and plants she learnt about when she studied horticulture.

For years my parents were involved in Save Albert Park, a campaign that aimed to relocate the Formula 1 Grand Prix from a public parkland to a permanent track. Their activism and their love of the bush provided me with a strong environmental and social consciousness that I only really began to explore when I moved to Daylesford from Melbourne at 31, following my older sister Kate who had moved there several years earlier.

Daylesford was the first place I had lived on my own, and was the first time that I had given any proper thought to what kind of person I wanted to be and what kind of life I wanted to lead. Before then, I had been happy bumming around from share-house to share-house, working as a writer and editor, always saving to travel overseas. Although I spent the majority of these trips in big cities, unpacking my boxes in the small country town of my new house felt like my first ever homecoming. I loved the simplicity of a house on the edge of the bush.

I love that about camping too, the lack of boundary between inside and outside, and how brave it feels to sleep under the stars in summer and crawl into the womb of a tent when it's cold. I love cooking in a billy and my hair always smelling of smoke. I love dirt under my fingernails. I'm not too fussed by snakes, spiders and little crawly things, so long as they stay outside the tent. I love how intrepid I always feel with my head torch on, or having to use my pocketknife or dig a hole to go to the toilet.

Planting the seed

But every single night? I had never seen Zephyr so excited. He started sleeping in his sleeping bag to prepare for the adventure.

'Haven't you always wanted to live in a tent, Meg?' he said, attempting to convince me that a cubby-house-sized home was preferable to any other kind.

'I do like the idea of living outside and not having to clean up after you,' I retorted, squeezing his shoulder.

I said it as a joke, but once the words were out I could feel something inside begin to shift. I felt both tense with excitement and light with the promise of change.

'I won't have to remind you a hundred times to close the front door. I won't have to scrub the black ring from the bath after you've been in it. And I won't have to remind you to flush the toilet after you've done a poo. Oh yeah! Count me in!'

These were said in jest, but they were also very appealing. No floors to sweep, no dishwasher to unstack, no walking around the house turning off lights, no tripping over books in the hallway, no scrubbing the rug under the kitchen table to remove hardening bits of porridge, no cleaning toothpaste spray from the bathroom mirror, no wiping pumpkin soup and pasta sauce and dried milk from the stovetop. There would be other chores, new jobs and duties that go hand in hand with being a parent and with life on the road. Did it matter where we were?

For the past several years we had immersed ourselves in volunteer roles. Helping to set up and maintain the day-to-day running of our town's community gardens was a major commitment. I was also on the committee of the local food co-op, on the International Women's Day organising committee, on the Neighbourhood Centre committee of management, and working with the Hepburn Relocalisation Network, a group that organises events to help prepare our shire for the twin challenges of peak oil and climate change.

We were also a soccer household. Patrick and Zeph played, Patrick coached Zeph's team and was also on the club's organising committee and I made food for the canteen.

We loved being able to contribute our time and energy to the various community groups and seeing the changes our efforts made.

But we felt suffocated by routine. With home-educating Zeph, Patrick finishing his doctorate, my completing a draft of my first manuscript, a new baby, and working a combined 40 hours a week as volunteers, we were absolutely wrung out.

And more than ready to untie ourselves.

Preparations

— Patrick —

With the decision made, I now had the focus to finish my thesis. But on top of a relentless workload of endnotes and final edits there was much to do to prepare for our big trip.

Money. We didn't need much, but we weren't going anywhere unless our little mortgage was being paid off. We oscillated between selling up and renting. In one of our swings to sell, we had the house valued, but our property's green credentials held little value with the local real-estate agents. Walking around with their clipboards they wanted to see and tick off double garages, reverse-cycle air conditioners and multiple bedrooms and bathrooms.

'Where are the boxes for things that bring down household waste and running costs?' I asked one agent. 'Swales, food forests, chicken palaces, double-glazing, rainwater tanks, solar panels, food cellars, bike storage and compost bays?'

I could see him thinking what's up with this hippie,

so we stuck with the plan to rent the house, and decided to be our own agents. A few times we doubted our decision to leave at all, but the idea of adventure was sticky and difficult to throw off. After tidying the house and photographing every room, we wrote a brief spiel about its best features. It was such a great house – small and easy to clean and heat, and close to town, the food co-op, cinema, library, op shops, the community food gardens, the lake and forests to forage in.

We posted the pics and blurb on our blog, shared them on Facebook and hoped for the best.

The next day the enquiries began. And after a few weeks we had a number of families interested. Making the choice was going to be difficult. We'd never been a landlord or landlady before, and the idea was as unappealing as private property itself. We had taken on debt and become landowners because the tourist town in which we live had created an impossibly expensive rental market, favouring tourists for weekend hires. The monthly rent was fairly similar to a small mortgage, and we knew once our trees had deep roots and were bearing fruit and our poultry system was set up, it would be as cheap (or as expensive) to service a mortgage.

At the time we made the decision to buy, Meg had a full-time job working from home, editing website content for an internet company, without which we would never have been loaned a cent.

My worldview wasn't exactly geared to establishing a credit rating. I had pretty much worked for myself

Preparations

since I was twenty-one, selling books and knick-knacks at markets, doing gardening and building work, and occasionally selling my drawings, prints and paintings. Otherwise, I took on short-term hospitality work. I had a dozen super funds, all with less than $200 in them. I would feed the paperwork that came through the snail mail to the worm farm, thinking my retirement fund should amount to about $1000, and when I get sick and elderly I'd take myself off into the bush like an old dog and self-compost somewhere peaceful. Not only did our home have little status in the big grown-up world of household consumption, our form of economics also didn't rate.

The day we signed the mortgage, the company Meg worked for went broke. When Meg was phoned by a fellow worker I watched her expression change as she listened. I thought someone had died.

'Fuuuuck,' Meg looked ashen.

She relayed the news. We both looked at each other in horror as reality set in, before bursting into laughter. Not that we ever told the lender. Until I was awarded the scholarship to do my doctorate a few years later, paying the instalments was difficult. We would get a phone call every fortnight reminding us our payments were late. Our loose, free-dragging honeymoon period as a couple lapsed into a few hard years of money woes. I was kicking myself once again for being trapped inside a monetary cage. My newfound sense of liberty was again under threat as I dragged myself between one bloody miserable building site to another, chasing up payments, trying to complete a week's work in just a few days in order to get the repayment in on time.

While everybody who came to see our home was more than suitable, one particular family from Melbourne stood out. They had been wanting to try out life in the country before making the move permanent. They were also friends of friends, so it felt like an easy decision. It was only one item checked from a long list of things to do, but it was a big one.

We relaxed somewhat, even though the most vital details of the trip – how we'd travel and where we'd go – were not yet resolved and we'd given ourselves just four months to prepare. It seems funny now to realise that back then we hadn't yet finalised how we would travel. Initially we toyed with the idea of walking. We would push Woody in a homebuilt pram-like wagon that would carry him and a considerable amount of our gear. Or maybe we would take two wagons?

'Perhaps we could take a horse and dray and walk alongside?' I threw into the mix one night over dinner.

Zeph's eleven-year-old eyes lit up. 'Yeah! You guys could walk alongside and Woody and I could take the reins.'

We all laughed, including one-year-old Woody, hearing his name used so excitedly by his older brother. This made us all laugh harder and Zero started barking and jumping around, giving Zeph cause to say, 'This is it, this is it, that's how we'll travel!'

Preparations

'Woah, slow down mister,' I quickly interjected. If it had just been us two adults it would have been easier to make the decision, but a family of so many differing abilities and needs was more complicated. Even though our aches and blisters and my cantankerous mood from our attempted hike to Melbourne were now rolled sweetly into distant memory, we still weren't game to try another walk, especially one of this scale, even with a horse and a dray.

We also contemplated taking public transport. Again there was the matter of carrying all our gear, and the question of how far we'd be able to explore a region limited by train and bus lines. But the most important factor was Zero, who would not be allowed to travel with us. We had smuggled him on public transport a few times before: in a box, in Woody's baby carrier and in a sports bag, feeding him pumpkin seeds to keep him quiet. But what would happen if we were caught? Come home and camp in a friend's backyard? We wouldn't kick out our tenants at short notice.

We considered hitch-hiking, something I'd done a lot of in my late teens and early twenties. I loved the chance encounters and the conversations with people who were kind enough to stop. Meg had also had positive experiences. About ten years ago she had travelled to New Zealand for a two-week break and stayed six months, WWOOFing (Willing Workers on Organic Farms) and hitching around the south island, and generally drifting, sleeping under bridges and on beaches. She intermittently travelled with others she'd met and loved the idea of travelling in the same way again. But we could see how people might be reluctant to pick up so many of us.

Not long after we moved into our house I built a carport on the western side for our then remaining car. It was like a giant shutter that blocked out the harsh afternoon sun from coming into the house in the summer months, with a roof to catch precious rainwater. After we sold the car and upgraded our ordinary treadlies to long-tailed cargo bikes, I enclosed the structure with rammed earthen walls to make a workshop and bike-parking area Meg dubbed the bikeport. We dug up the driveway and planted it with fruit trees, blocking off cars from entering the property. We were a committed bicycle family now and travelling Australia by these simple freedom machines made the most sense. We could carry our camping gear, food, water and heavy baby, and we could take Zero.

From the first day he joined our family at eleven weeks of age, Zero came with us wherever we went. If we walked, we carried him in our jackets, or he trotted along beside us. And if we biked, he rode in a basket at the front. He jumped out a couple of times, but didn't like the feeling of hitting the bitumen or nearly being ridden over, so he learned to stay, leaning to the side around corners, sitting on the downhill swoops, and standing with his two front paws on the edge of the basket on the uphills. We considered not taking him with us, but not for long. We had friends who would look after him, but we didn't like the idea of him being left alone while

Preparations

his minders were at work or school. A Jack Russell is a particularly sensitive being. We wouldn't leave one of our human kin behind, so really, we couldn't leave our dog either. This meant we would be limited in terms of where we could go. We couldn't visit national parks or certain beaches for example, but it was a concession worth making if it meant having Zero close.

Deciding to travel by bicycle meant we could travel the highways and we could go off-road. We could travel 5 kilometres a day or 50. We could travel inland or we could hug the coastline. We could even take a train if it came to that, and smuggle Zero if we really had to. If we were caught and thrown off, we still had our bikes.

It was easy to wrap a puppy in a blanket and carry him in a bike basket, but a baby was somewhat harder. In Australia, anyway. In Asian countries you see bikes and motorbikes struggling under the weight of entire families, piled high with people and belongings, babies strapped to the backs of side-saddling mothers, not a helmet in sight, the traffic maintaining its own logic. When Woody was first born, we walked with him everywhere in a baby carrier and researched all the different ways of carrying babies on bikes. When at four months of age he was old enough to hold up his head, we settled on an enclosed trailer that we could pull behind our bikes. But when the trailer was fully loaded with baby, library books, bulk oats and grains from the food co-op, roadside fruit and Zero, it was hard to pull. Not just because of the weight, but because the drag was considerable. The trailer was ideal for its carrying capacity over short distances provided we didn't overload it, but on long trips it was too much hard work. And also dangerous.

On the roads with little shoulder, when our bikes were safely off the bitumen, the wider trailer would sometimes sit out, exposing Woody to greater danger. And what would we do if we had to catch a train? Our bikes are longer than regular bikes, and with the trailer attached they would take up too much room in a carriage. All this led to us deciding to travel with a baby seat on the back of one of the bikes.

We'd also decided to travel north, leaving in late spring. We'd follow the sun and place no other restrictions on our journey other than to join my family for Christmas in New South Wales. Then we just wanted to stray and not be held to timeframes, expectations or destinations, and find out just how far we could push low-consumption living on the road.

The next bike decision involved Zeph.

Mel, now known in our household as Aunty Mel, was as excited as we were for Zeph to accompany us on such a trip, at least for half the year. As an experienced traveller herself, born in Japan and raised in several countries, she knew that travel would be a positive form of education for her son. We started thinking about the most environmental way he would travel to and from home and what his wheels were going to be when he was riding with us. The problem was we didn't know where we'd be when it was time for the changeover. We

Preparations

conceded that he'd probably have to fly to meet us.

Zeph was set on having his own wheels, and we thought about him having a folding bike that he would bring along with his backpack, but at age eleven we were not ready to trust him riding busy roads solo, even sandwiched between Meg and me. He was a strong rider but Australian roads are dangerous and his boy brain sometimes a little too loose.

Meg had grown up on the back of her father's tandem, regularly going on the Great Victorian Bike Ride. A tandem was the obvious solution, which one of us adults could ride solo and even pick up hitchhikers when Zeph was not with us. We sourced an ex-hire tandem in Melbourne and Meg and Zeph jumped on enthusiastically, but found it unruly and too big to manage. So we decided to have Zero upfront as navigator, Zeph on the back as co-pedaller and me steering the long ship from the middle. I sold my long-tail ute bike to pay for it.

Our final configuration: five mammals, two bikes.

At this stage of the planning I was sweating on my doctorate. When I wasn't at one of the community-garden handover discussions, soccer-club committee meetings, coaching the under-11s, playing in the seniors or organising some aspect of our trip, I was locked in our bedroom writing, with Meg keeping guard at the door and letting no one in. It was no wonder we needed to get away.

As an appendix to my thesis, which was simply called 'Walking for Food', I included a list of over 100 species of plants, mushrooms and animals that we had slowly incorporated into our diet, which we had walked, foraged, hunted and fished for. When our winter produce garden was in low productivity we foraged the old medicinal weeds of Europe and beyond that had come with colonisation. These free food-medicines constituted 5 to 10 per cent of our diet. They supplemented other free foods from our home and community gardens, as well as bought bulk food from two local co-ops, a small produce shop and nearby family farms.

We recognised that to travel lightly we needed to extend our foraging knowledges as we moved into other climate zones and bio-regions. We decided that researching a book about free food was to become the central focus of our adventure – we wanted to show others just how much exists in Australia and draw attention to the edible and medicinal weeds brought by European agriculture, as much as traditional bush tuckers and medicines. The book was to be called *Free Tucker*, which we are still working on. None of the species we collected required cultivation or money markets. They were truly autonomous, free to live, reproduce and procure.

We still, however, required some dollars. Our knowledge was not that advanced to simply live from the land, but we also knew that such dedication to practising the art of free food for an extended period would probably increase it dramatically.

We started a crowd-funding campaign to raise

Preparations

money for some of our equipment. We aimed for $3000 and by the time the campaign ended we'd raised almost $4000. We were now set to order ten waterproof panniers, front-wheel bike racks, hiking-weight rain jackets, zero-degree down sleeping bags, bike lights and a host of other smaller items such as a root-vegetable foraging tool, a small hatchet and lightweight pruning saw. We considered taking two of our hens in a small enclosed basket, free-ranging them whenever we stopped. But Meg and I were already outnumbered by children and a little animal, and thought it wise not to complicate things further. We'd look for happy free-ranging hens on the road and knock on doors to inquire whether we could buy half a dozen eggs. We had sun-dried hundreds of plums and wild apples the previous autumn and still had a good bank of them.

Nappies were another matter. Produce no waste is a major tenet of permaculture, a principle that we now wholeheartedly applied to our lives. We didn't think we could manage with cloth nappies, which were easy to handle in a home environment. Meg found online a Tasmanian company producing 100 per cent compostable nappies. Bloody expensive, but we could dig holes and bury them along the way. We ordered a box to carry and sent another box ahead to my brother's home in NSW. We avoided most eco-products. We agreed with the English writer George Monbiot that they were just another expanding market doing little to mitigate global consumption. After the two boxes ran out we'd see what else we could find. In the meantime we would attempt a form of early toilet training called elimination communication, where the parent or caregiver develops a critical and intuitive understanding of the child's bodily needs, which helps the child urinate or defecate somewhere favourable, thus avoiding the need to buy nappies or be laundry slaves. We were going to be living outdoors and heading into the warmer parts of the country, so there'd be plenty of opportunities for Woody to be nappy-free.

Once we started amassing all our equipment we began going on practice rides. The bikes were becoming considerably heavier with all the gear and we were beginning to worry we'd be pushing them up every hill. Ordinarily, a cycle-tourist carries only his or her own gear, but Meg and I were also carrying for others.

We searched online for families touring Australia on bikes and found absolutely nothing. We couldn't believe it. We went further afield and found families in Canada and America and scoured their blogs for clues on how to handle the weight. We started to consider some electrical assistance for the hills and found a guy on the Ballarat Permaculture Guild Facebook page who was just starting up a little e-bike business.

Sam, who ironically has a day job in the automobile industry, got involved in e-bikes to reduce his family's carbon output. He recognised the need for transition from car to bike culture, but that not everyone is an Olympian and so e-bikes became his sensible middle ground. He became an enthusiastic patron of our trip and offered to set up both bikes for just the cost of the hardware. Our 20- to 40-kilometre practice rides became immediately more manageable and even though we had no idea how we would recharge the batteries on the road, we knew they'd make the ascents more rideable.

About a month before we were due to leave, two cycle-tourers came for lunch before their book launch at our local bookshop. Sophie and Greg had cycled from Tasmania to Cairns, visiting sustainability pioneers along the way, and Greg had turned their experiences into the book *Changing Gears*. They recommended we get helmet mirrors to help us develop a defensive riding habit. They told us we could better anticipate when to get off the road without looking around and tipping the balance of our heavy bikes. We'd done enough riding on a range of busy roads to know just how invaluable these mirrors would be.

Bike maintenance knowledge was something Meg and I were a little light on. I barely knew how to repair a puncture. I didn't even know there was a right or wrong way to put on a tyre, that you have to follow the arrowing tread. Our friend Nick, who had toured Australia extensively on a bicycle and who at Meg's invitation (when she worked there) took regular bicycle maintenance workshops at the Daylesford Neighbourhood Centre, was just the right teacher. With some of our crowdfunded money we were able to hire Nick, who took us through the basics of gear cable maintenance, replacing disc brake pads, cleaning and oiling chains and sprockets, and changing a tyre.

'I'm heading out a complete bicycle novice, Nick, but I aim to come back a bike mechanic,' I told him as

I watched his technique of ragging down the chain to remove the excess oil he'd applied to it.

Nick suggested taking a small section of chain and a chain breaker, which we included in our toolkit. Also a short section of hard rubber in case one of our tyres got a tear in the middle of nowhere – advice I neglected to follow, for which I kicked myself almost a year later.

'There will be times when you just want to find a shed somewhere and put the bike away for a few weeks, and never look at it,' he said with a knowing expression.

While we worked, a grin came and went on his face, like he was recalling events from his trips. I saw both glee and horror.

Jesus, what are we getting ourselves into?

Among the last things to prepare were the house and garden. We held a garage sale and purged ourselves of many unnecessary things, including parts of our libraries. What didn't sell we donated to one of the local op-shops. Our small garden love-shack – which usually serves as accommodation for SWAPs (our acronym for Social Warming Artists and Permaculturalists, a version of WWOOFs) – became home to all our earthly belongings, mostly taken up by beds, books, a couch, kitchen table and chairs. We sensed that after a year of living in a tent with a billy and a few bowls for a kitchen, we'd balk at having to unpack and face all the accumulations of modern life.

I gave the garden a two-year prune, and deeply

Preparations

mulched all the perennial food beds with well-rotted wood-chips, leaf litter and whatever organic matter I could get my hands on – I just wanted it to survive the heat of summer. We couldn't expect our tenants to pay as much attention to the garden as we did. Six months earlier Zeph had planted a year's supply of garlic as one of his home-ed projects, which we dug up and cellared, taking about thirty heads with us and leaving the rest as a gift for our tenants-to-be.

About a week out from leaving we began to breathe more deeply. We were pretty much ready. Zero was staying close to us, observing our panniers amassing at the front door, afraid he was going to be left behind.

'No way, little dog,' I reassured him. 'We're not leaving you.'

With such excitement in the house, and with the required copies of my doctorate finally posted, something changed in me again. All of a sudden I was finished with one big project and immediately confronting the next. I had neglected to leave some time for a break. On top of this I now had the space to face my fears, or at least acknowledge their existence.

'I keep getting visions of us getting slammed by a truck,' I said to Meg one night, unable to keep it to myself any longer.

'Me too,' she said, looking at me gravely.

In sharing our fears they multiplied.

What the hell were we doing? We proceeded to work ourselves into a state. We were sure we were going to kill our kids on these totally unsuitable roads for bicycles. No wonder we couldn't find any information about families doing this in Australia. It was madness. We both hadn't felt so permanently sick in our stomachs since we watched the documentary *The world according to Monsanto*, about what one very powerful company had in mind for the future of the world's food supply.

Each night I'd wake in a sweat with the image of Meg and Woody being taken out by a road train, or something similar happening to Zeph. Jesus! I could never forgive myself if they were killed. I'd have to spend the remainder of my life drinking myself to death, hiding from Mel and Meg's family. It would be my fault; it was my idea.

In that last week, Meg was interviewed by Megan Spencer on ABC regional radio about how she was feeling about the trip.

'I'm petrified!' she confessed. 'I'm worried about slipping on gravel, being hit by a semi-trailer, crazy weather, P-platers texting on their phones and taking us out, getting really sunburnt and running out of water.'

With the house packed up and empty we threw a party to say goodbye to our loved ones. It was just the antidote to stem the sick feeling we couldn't quite throw. I joked with some mates about becoming flattened fauna and, as everybody at the party except for us were car users, I provocatively added that Australian roads won't become safe for non-polluters unless more of us were riding on them. I was sure our friends weren't going to miss my environmental sermonising.

Our friend Alison came over the next day and

Preparations

helped us clean the house for its new family. Together we washed away the stains of our life; the party, the kids running the garden into the floorboards, the food and booze spills of laughing, spluttering adults and the mud-clad dogs.

We spent our last night in our emptied out home as though it was already a tent, lying on our blow-up mats trying to court sleep, feeling a mix of dreadful foreboding and restless excitement.

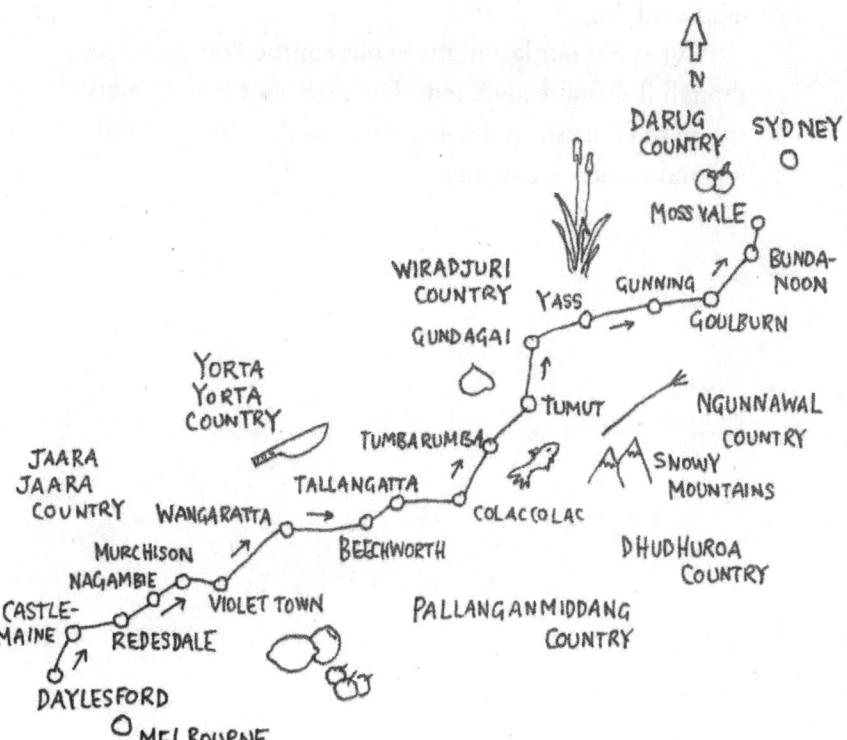

On the road

– Meg –

DAYLESFORD to MOSS VALE
1000 KILOMETRES
15 November 2013 to 22 December 2013

Two years before our trip, my sister Kate, her husband and their three daughters left Daylesford for a six-month adventure driving up the centre of Australia and down the west coast. An hour after we waved them off, they pulled over to see how the vintage caravan they were towing was faring. They opened the door to find a big glass jar had fallen and smashed, the interior covered in flour.

'We had no idea how to pack a caravan,' Kate laughed. 'To this day you can still find flour in the cracks and under the lino.'

The start of our adventure was equally inauspicious. After we said our goodbyes to our chooks and ducks, and to our friends Jeff and Cath who had brought around lunch, we swept the floors one more time and hid the keys for our tenants who were arriving the following afternoon. We pushed our bikes up the path and stood out on our quiet road.

There we were. We were really doing this. No more items to tick off lists, no more packing and weighing, unpacking and labelling panniers and wondering if two t-shirts each was enough. No more handover meetings for our various community commitments, no more goodbye visits to my grandfather in Melbourne, no more last-minute notes with instructions for our tenants about how to pump rainwater from the small house tank to the main one.

We were ready. We put on our helmets, adjusted our mirrors and pedalled up the hill, singing loudly as our heavy bikes creaked along in time. We didn't want a big farewell on the day, but we had arranged to stop off briefly at the community garden next to the library to say one last goodbye to some friends who couldn't make it to our party, to my parents, and to meet our friend Clay, who would ride with us some of the way that afternoon.

Patrick was on the tandem without his co-pedaller, just Zero in the basket upfront. After many conversations with Mel we decided that we would leave on 15 November and Zeph would drive with her parents to meet us six weeks later in Moss Vale, in the NSW Southern Highlands. They were spending Christmas with family in Sydney, and we were going to spend it with Patrick's. Zeph would then ride with us for three months, go back to Mel for the soccer season, then return to us for the final three months. It was a lot of backwards and forwards but it was a solution that everybody, especially Zeph, was happy with. At the same time, Zeph had mixed feelings about not joining us from the start. He said that he was sad to be missing out, but was also not sorry to skip six weeks of hard work and the potential stresses that might arise until we found our cycle-touring rhythm. I knew how he felt.

In my twenties and thirties I travelled the world on my own. I rented apartments in New York, Berlin, Tokyo and Bangkok, twice I went to the Burning Man festival in the Black Rock Desert, Nevada. I hitchhiked around Canada and New Zealand, I taught English in Laos. I shaved my head and painted on facial hair while travelling in southern India after arriving at night with no money and nowhere to stay. I had magic mushrooms in Osaka, opium in Laos, ecstasy in San Francisco, smoked heroin in Thailand and ice in New York. I knew what risks were; I knew the smell and shape and colour of danger. I knew how to take care of myself and, most importantly, I knew how to trust myself, and to embrace the mistakes I had made.

But this was different. This wasn't just shunning routine. This wasn't just letting your kids stay up late and eat cereal for dinner. This was consciously putting your kids in the path of continual uncertainty. On my own I felt intrepid and daring, but as a mother I felt less willing to let go of the familiar.

That November afternoon was a cold one. We were

wearing jackets and long pants, and I also had a skirt on over the top to hide the padded bulky bum of my bike nix. We had bought the shorts for the trip because we were told they prevented chafing, but felt a thousand kilometres away from the lycra aesthetic. I stopped at the intersection across the road from the community garden to let a car pass. My folks were already there, talking to Patrick who had arrived a minute earlier.

And down I went. Somehow my skirt got caught over the back of my seat, meaning the bike was stopped but I couldn't get off to put my feet on the ground. I didn't fall in slow motion; I fell hard and fast. At 80 kilograms, including Woody and gear, and me only 50, my bike was too heavy and cumbersome to lift on my own. Luckily my panniers were so full that Woody, strapped into his seat, didn't touch the ground. He started howling, although he wasn't hurt; he was just responding to my panicked screams to Patrick to come and help me. This was no smashed jar of flour hidden within the walls of a caravan, but a very public, very humiliating, very noisy beginning to our trip. If I couldn't make it up the street, what chance in hell did I have of being able to ride my bike for a year?

I was crying, Woody was crying and Patrick was waiting for cars to go by so he could come and help us. It was embarrassing enough that I had to wait for him to come and rescue me, but with my parents watching too?

I felt utterly deflated. Two kind women came running, but the bike was too heavy for them to lift. Once Patrick had helped us over the road, my parents hugged

Woody and me, and then my mum stood stroking my hair while I sat on a concrete step breastfeeding her distressed grandson. If she thought I was an unfit mother for going on such a trip, she didn't say anything.

And then Clay arrived and it was time to go. I wiped my tears on my dad's jumper as I hugged him goodbye, took my skirt off and stuffed it into my clothes pannier, strapped Woody into his seat, put our helmets on and away we went, dinging our bells until we were out of sight.

After about an hour of riding we stopped to say goodbye to Clay at Guildford, where Patrick also spotted some water ribbons, our first bush food for the trip. With our digging tool, he carefully unearthed from the water some small white rhizomes for us to try. We were looking forward to eating the autonomous foods we already knew, and adding to our *Free Tucker* collection as we rode up country. Recording a new species was usually a relatively simple task: identifying it by name and taking numerous photographs of its various parts. If we didn't know its name we'd do an image search online, typing in the key features, carry a sample and ask other people, or post a photo on our blog and ask our readers to help identify it. Once we had the name of the species we could then research its uses. While Patrick eagerly documented this first new plant for our collection, I was excitedly digging a hole to bury Woody's first compostable nappy.

We were already ahead of schedule. Not knowing how far we would be able to ride on a daily basis, we worked out that we had to average a mere 26 kilometres a day for six weeks to make it to Moss Vale in time to meet Zeph. We spent our first night in Castlemaine, 37 kilometres north of Daylesford, at our friends Tosh and Juliette's place. They were away but had kindly offered us their house. We felt exhausted from the build-up to our departure, and tired from the ride, but elated by the reality that we were finally on the road. Although it didn't yet feel like we were really on our way. We were treated to a home-cooked meal that night by our friends Lee and Dave, who came over with their kids. It was our final hoorah of familiarity.

We had pedalled to Castlemaine before but not beyond. When we packed up and left early the next day, we were finally out of our comfort zone. For the first time in years we didn't know what was around each corner. As Patrick was our navigator, he and Zero rode at the front. Usually we rode close together, but that day I hung back a little, needing my own space, my own thoughts. Although Woody was saying a few words, at 14 months, he couldn't yet hold a conversation. I chatted to him, describing what we were seeing, naming different birds, different trees. But for the most part I was hushed, focussing on my breath, the road, the land, the rhythm of my legs.

A tribe of white-winged choughs flying alongside us signalled our arrival into Redesdale, about 35 kilometres east of Castlemaine. It was a Saturday afternoon and the local tennis club was just winding down their weekly games. After everybody left we set up camp just

On the road

near the courts. It was a tiny town, but still it felt bold to unpack our shiny new bags and put up our tents in broad daylight. Instead of one large tent we had settled on two small hiking tents. One for Patrick and me and the other for Woody and Zero, and Zephyr when he joined us. After a simple pasta dish cooked in the billy on our lightweight gas burner, I put Woody to bed, hoping he would sleep through until morning.

Finding somewhere to pitch our tents each night and recharge our body batteries was one thing, but we also needed to find power to charge our electrical devices. We had looked into light and portable solar panels and dynamo-style rechargers for our bike batteries, phone, camera and laptop, but couldn't find anything suitable except a SolarMonkey that we bought but soon deemed to be expensive landfill. Sam, who had retrofitted our bikes with electric motors, had estimated that each bike battery used about 5 cents' worth of electricity to recharge. Even though we only used the motors on the hills, we charged them whenever we could, not knowing when we'd be near power again. We soon became experts at finding free power points, often concealed in public parks or recreation grounds. While Woody would sleep in the shade of a tree after lunch and we charged our devices, Patrick and I collected a bag of rubbish. We saw this as an informal gift exchange with the local community of wherever we happened to be. On one of these first days, when there wasn't much to collect, Patrick pruned a self-sown apple tree with our fold-up saw, as another form of barter.

If we had had a bigger saw we may have used it on the outskirts of Nagambie three days after we left home. We arrived just before dusk and quickly set up camp down a path leading to the Goulburn River. The moon was huge and bright, the mozzies fierce, and the stench of rubbish, sickly. It wasn't an ideal site but it was late and we were too tired to be fussy. I had just finished blowing up our sleeping mats when the wind picked up.

'Uh oh,' said Patrick.

I imagined he had seen or heard some drunks heading our way. There were empty bourbon cans crushed and scattered around and I thought we had perhaps encroached on a favourite watering hole. But the menace Patrick had noticed was a huge white gum that the increased wind had brought to his attention.

Woody was crying, we hadn't eaten dinner yet and the mozzies weren't retreating from the wind. But our tents had to be moved. It just wasn't a chance we were going to take. Several years earlier Patrick and I had been camping in the old crater of Lalgambook, renamed Mount Franklin by colonists, and had almost been crushed by a large limb of a poplar tree that had been rotted out by white ants and had missed our tent by only metres. At Lalgambook, frazzled in the middle of the night, we packed up our things and went home. In Nagambie, to the tune of our howling baby, we unpegged our tents and ferried our bags and bikes about 50 metres away. We were closer to the highway and our camp was more exposed, but the ground was flat and in the shadow of no tree.

On the road

Nick, our bike maintenance friend, had told us that when cycle-touring he always started looking for a campsite at around 2 pm, because it could take a while to find a desirable site. Two in the afternoon was sensible, but rarely achievable for us. That was usually when Woody napped, or when we were just getting on our bikes again after stopping for lunch. When we did manage the early arrival time, we were chuffed as it meant we had the rest of the afternoon to relax, to nap, to read, to fish or to make love while Woody slept.

Two days later, after setting up our tents early beside the Honeysuckle Creek, which ran through a public reserve in Violet Town, Patrick wrote in his journal while Woody and I napped. Later, we walked up to the Neighbourhood Centre and charged our batteries while we checked our emails and blogged. Our intention was to blog every ten days or so with anecdotes from the road, and chronicle all the different foods and medicines we were finding along the way.

We felt at home in Violet Town, 30 kilometres from Benalla. People walked their dogs past our rather public stealth camp and smiled and called out hello. We detected no fear of the interloper, which was different from how we felt in Nagambie and Murchison.

It was at the Neighbourhood Centre in Violet Town that we met Denise. She had just bought a new computer and was having difficulty setting it up. As I helped her, we talked about our journey.

'Please come for dinner tonight,' Denise insisted. 'I'd love to hear more.'

We were treated to a delicious home-cooked meal made with produce from her garden. We didn't know this then, but Denise's invitation was the first of many where strangers would surprise us with their kindness and, often, their home-grown produce. In our small hometown it had taken many years to become part of a greater network of support. After Woody was born this network set up a meal tree that lasted six weeks, meaning that for all that time we didn't need to cook a single dinner. Every time we left the house we would return to find a bag of hand-me-down clothes that someone had left on our doorstep for our new babe. Meeting Denise was our first experience of finding community and support on the road.

At the Winton wetlands, just south of Wangaratta, we met Gary and his grandson Josh as we were setting up camp in an all but abandoned caravan park. Since Lake Mokoan had been turned back into a wildlife and bird sanctuary wetland, water-skiing and motor-boating holiday-makers had been forced to indulge their passions elsewhere. Gary had been a permanent resident there since he got out of prison, he told us over the beers he brought down to share.

The public phone box just near where we pitched our tents had some time ago been smashed in and graffitied, the handset yanked out. The park was a grim environment, hot and full of old motor junk and rabbits. We were travelling with our bow and arrows for exactly such a situation, but Patrick was too tired to go hunting that night. There were only two or three permanent human residents and we still hadn't seen the owners when we turned off our head torches to go to sleep.

'How's Gary?' I whispered.

'A ripper!' Patrick mumbled, almost asleep. In the morning I discovered Patrick had slept with our small hatchet tucked under his mattress. He would do this often over the coming months, though thankfully only confide this to me in the morning.

The next day, after briefly meeting and paying the caravan park owners, we left the wetlands and set out for Wangaratta, cycling through Ned Kelly territory up into the Warby Ranges. At home, oaks, hawthorns, apples and blackberries have all formed ecological partnerships with blackwood wattles, peppermints and messmates, making habitat and food for various animals, including humans. In northern-central Victoria, we found that figs, walnuts and loquats were the naturalising trees. The figs and walnuts were not in season, but the loquats were. We filled our gobs and every spare space in our panniers with the yellow fleshy fruits.

We no longer felt the need to stop our bikes so often because our bums hurt. It took about a week for our sit bones to stop feeling bruised. At home we ate fermented foods – yoghurt, sauerkraut and pickled veggies – to keep our gut bacteria healthy, but on the road I took probiotic capsules and made sure I washed whenever I could to prevent thrush or a urinary tract infection, things that are not fun at any time, but particularly when you're living rough.

We did, however, stop our bikes often because we

could. We began to understand the possibilities of this gentle straying. We were ahead of schedule for our Moss Vale rendezvous so we didn't feel rushed, and because we were riding, and I was breastfeeding, we were always hungry. Even after seeing thousands of fruit-laden plants, our excitement never waned. All forms of citrus, black nightshade berries, cherry plums and many more loquats were collected and devoured as our northerly transit ripened these sugary gifts.

Woody became our chief spotter. While Patrick and I were pedalling and watching the traffic and hazards of the road, Woody would point and call out, 'More, more!' when he spied a tree in fruit. Later, as his language and identification skills developed, he would call out the name of the fruits he saw and, to our amazement, the name of the trees when they weren't in fruit or flower.

Those first few weeks were a period of adjustment for all of us. More than when we were at home, I was aware how my emotional wellbeing was directly tied to my physical needs. If I felt safe on the roads, if my appetite and thirst were satiated, if I felt secure going to sleep, and if I didn't feel overwhelmed by all the daily unknowns of travel, I was happy. Although I was responsible for my own wellbeing on my own bike, I felt that I was putting much of my safety in Patrick's hands. By day he was our navigator determining the best route, and by night he was our protector, helped out by Zero in the other tent, who would bark to alert us if he heard a noise nearby. I also had my own knife, and felt certain that if my family were threatened I would know what to do.

On the road

Woody adjusted to life on the road by staying as close to me as possible. On the bike was easy, but off the bike was more difficult. He only stopped grizzling when he was on top of me, meaning I couldn't do much, except sit with him on my knee while Patrick put up both tents, made dinner, and turned our nightly campsite into our home. I could have put Woody down and let him cry it out, but we were practising our version of attachment parenting, a philosophy that encourages a hands-on, nurturing approach. It was frustrating, but we knew it was a phase that wouldn't last forever.

Woody also had to learn how to fall asleep upright in his bike seat. Riding after lunch, I would feel him slump to one side. The first time it happened, I looked in my helmet mirror and when I couldn't see my little passenger I panicked, thinking he had fallen off. But he had become a loquat fiend. Eaten in quantity, loquats have a gentle but noticeable sedative effect, especially on fast metabolisms. We would often save them up for just before his naptime.

On the rail trail from Wangaratta to Beechworth, mulberries were in season and we came across old public trees. We had never ridden on a rail trail before, and had no idea that the disused train lines, with their slight inclines and lack of cars and trucks, could be so pleasurable. Zero was happy too, taking off to chase rabbits or running along beside us.

Having climbed 300 metres above sea level over the last 15 kilometres of the trail, we were exhausted. We explored the touristy township of Beechworth a little, picked up some bread, oats and pasta and set up camp for a few days along Spring Creek near the centre of town, among the willows, gums and she-oaks. Just as fruit trees were proving to be essential for our appetites, stands of trees and bushes were proving to be essential for our stealthy home-making. In non-built up areas we could camp anywhere, beside creeks or streams and later on, beaches, or behind municipal toilet blocks. Before we left, one of my concerns had been where we would camp each night. Just as finding food to eat was turning out to be a daily treasure hunt, so too was locating the ideal campsite. Writer Tristan Gooley describes the unique skill of natural navigation as 'the rare art of finding your way using nature, including the sun, moon, stars, weather, land, sea, plants and animals'.

Being able to read the land does not mean that you necessarily understand cartography or geology or that you can follow the instructions of a GPS or compass. It is elemental, a kind of living literacy, a deep philosophical as well as practical understanding of country. The ability to find the perfect campsite was a talent of Patrick's that I was in awe of. We were intentionally travelling without a compass or guidebook, trusting instead in Patrick's intuition and his capacity to read the land. Even after months of studying how he found each site, I was unable to master the skill. In all the time we were away, I suggested only half a dozen sites that we actually set up camp in.

My skill was scavenging. And because I was always hungry, it was a skill I was always calling on and improving. At the Beechworth community garden, we watered thirsty plants and weeded over-crowded garden beds in exchange for some produce for dinner. I located in one of the compost bays some discarded capsicum, beans and tomatoes that I excitedly uncovered, and after washing them and cutting off the rotten bits, added them to our dinner. It was the first, but not last, time I would rummage for good tucker in a waste bin.

After Beechworth we pedalled 20 kilometres to Yackandandah and on to another rail trail at Huon, which took us over Lake Hume and into the windy, dusty town of Tallangatta. Decades ago, my uncles Ivan and John owned and ran the motel there, so I made a beeline for it. Even though the old building didn't look at all familiar, I still felt a connection with the town we had visited often when I was a kid.

It was late afternoon when we pulled over in a residential street to check our map. A man in a nearby house was on his veranda putting up his Christmas lights.

'You guys right?' he called out.

A few minutes later George and his partner Laura had invited us to camp in their backyard, take a shower and join them and their kids for spag bol. It was the first time we had been invited to stay overnight with a family. Even though we were loving free camping, we readily accepted their kind invitation.

After his shower though, Patrick questioned our hasty decision. Coming out of the bathroom, clean for the first time in days, he found George sitting on his bed sharpening a giant pig knife, looking up at Patrick with an odd expression. Woody and I were oblivious; we were outside bottle-feeding our hosts' baby under their laden lemon tree. But I knew something was up when I saw Patrick's ashen face when he came out to us. I was instantly alert.

'Check this out,' said George, following Patrick with the knife in hand. 'Come and check out my shed.'

One by one George displayed for us his sharpest knives, axes, guns and chainsaws while he told us the story of his earlier years. At fifteen he had been kicked out of school and initiated into a notorious Albury bikie gang. Four years later he managed to leave the gang, which was when he started a family with Laura. George was baby-faced, but also wise beyond his years. He was funny and sweet and an affectionate partner and father. I could see Patrick relaxing.

'I'm nineteen now and I reckon I've lived enough life for two lives,' he told us as he sharpened my pocketknife in his shed. 'Now I'm ready for just one long quiet one.'

That night the two dads went out fishing. George confessed that he'd never met a greenie before.

The next morning we began our climb into Snowy River country. We stopped at the Koetong Hotel for lunch and continued our sweaty ascent back on the rail trail to the former Shelley Station, which at 779 metres above sea level is the highest railway station ever built in Victoria. It was just after we stopped to take our photo at the old station sign that things got a little hairy.

All our unrealised fears of seeing George with his weapons the night before came back to haunt us. But this time it wasn't ex-bikies and pig knives that had us on edge, but the wild dogs George had warned us about that lived in the state forest.

The trail around Shelley wasn't finished yet; the rocks on the path were more suited to mountain bikes than our heavy road rides. We were keen to get off the track and veered onto a road that we thought would take us back onto the Murray Valley Highway. This road wasn't shown on any of our paper maps. We found ourselves winding deeper and deeper into a warren of unmarked pine plantation truck roads. It was mid-afternoon and I was getting seriously scared we'd have to spend the night in the forest. I was envisaging a mangy, slavering showdown around every bend. As it was getting serious, we called on Google Maps to help us. But Patrick was soon swearing at the app while looking at the sun's arc and trying to listen for the highway. My electric motor was down to its last bar of power, which I was saving for the emergency I knew was coming.

Like a scene from a spooky movie, I saw a shadow of a dog slink across the road on the crest of the hill we'd just come down. If we could have gone another way we would have, but the only route left to us was to backtrack.

'Whatever you do,' Patrick said soberly, 'do not stop pedalling. If your battery conks out just keep going.'

We readied ourselves and took off, riding our hearts out. At the top of the hill the dog was nowhere to be seen, but that could have been because I rode that short stretch with my eyes closed. After half an hour of frantic pedalling we were finally back on the highway. I had never felt so elated to see bitumen. After several kilometres we stopped in Berringama, relieved to be out of the dog woods, and rested in the old community hall. We leant our bikes against a road sign and I cried as Patrick held me. I didn't know it at the time, but they were not to be the last tears of the day.

The temperature that afternoon had been glorious, around 26°C, only now it was starting to get cold. It had already been a huge day and we were ready to set up camp but couldn't find anywhere suitable. We had been told of a caravan park at Colac Colac, only 20 kilometres away, which seemed within reach. I knew it would be slow going as my bike battery had run out, but I didn't mind. We trudged up and flew down a number of hills, then about 10 kilometres out from Colac Colac Patrick pulled over.

'My chain's come off. Keep going, I'll catch you up.'

After riding on for a while I realised that Patrick wasn't following us and I knew something was wrong. In preparing for the trip we had bought ourselves a secondhand smartphone, which was in my handlebar bag. Even though it was temperamental, Patrick had brought along his ten-year-old dumbphone that could be used to receive calls in an emergency. I called and called, but it was turned off. I rode on as slowly as I could, thinking that I might see Patrick and Zero in my helmet mirror any moment now, but I saw nothing, only the occasional car. I thought about stopping one and asking the driver if they had seen a man and a

On the road

dog on a bike, but I didn't like the idea of someone not very nice knowing that I was all alone out there with my baby, even though it was pretty bloody obvious. Instead I thought I would pedal to Colac Colac and find someone there to help me.

Woody started to cry and then I did too. I kept stopping to call Patrick. Why the fuck wasn't he turning his phone on? Getting lost trying to leave Shelley had used up all my patience and I was starting to lose my cool. I rode on, stopped to call, swore and cried, rode on. Over and over. Until finally, *finally* Patrick answered his phone. Being an old model, it relied on old technology and it had been out of range until then. Patrick found that more than the chain slipping, the rear wheel axle had broken, or rather, what we discovered later, the cassette pawls in the rear axle had become mangled. It was the first serious bike issue of our trip.

On I rode towards Colac Colac, while Patrick walked his bike and rolled it down any descent he could. It was starting to get dark and I needed to turn on my lights, though there was nowhere suitable for me to lean my heavy bike, so I just kept going. Soon enough there were more tears, but this time from relief on seeing the sign for the caravan park. Ten minutes later Woody and I were riding with Phil, the park's owner, in his ute as we went back to find Patrick and Zero.

After setting up camp in the dark, we made a quick dinner of pasta, garlic, dandelion greens, olive oil, salt and pepper, then collapsed onto our mats and slept for nearly ten hours. The next morning Phil very kindly made some calls, and Patrick arranged to courier his wheel to a bike shop in Albury.

We were looking at five days, they told us. Five days! We were ahead of schedule though five days was really going to set us back. We had no choice but to embrace the situation, and given how idyllic it was there, it wasn't going to be difficult.

The Corryong Creek that ran alongside the caravan park grounds was pristine. We fished, swam, giggled at our bike shorts tan lines, spotted large pregnant crayfish, and spent much time talking with John and Jenny, who were camped just near us in their caravan. They were the first grey nomads we met who showered us with grandparent-like generosity with tea and cake and the use of a bicycle for Patrick so we could all ride into Corryong, 7 kilometres away.

Our 'forced' stay in Colac Colac taught us the valuable lesson that difficult situations dovetail into good things.

The day we left we had to learn that lesson again. Patrick's electric motor was becoming more and more temperamental, and then cut out halfway up a steep incline not far from Towong and the New South Wales border. The cattle grazing nearby were treated to a real show, as Patrick filled the morning air with extensive expletives.

Sixty kilometres from the border, and after spending our first wet night camped at Paddys Creek, we arrived in the timber town of Tumbarumba. Just as we did in Beechworth we set up camp in a park near the centre of town among a dense planting of melaleucas. By day, with flags and lights and high-vis vests, we tried to make ourselves as visible as possible on the roads, while at night we made ourselves disappear. We left our hidden campsite each morning and spent our days waiting for a new controller for Patrick's electric motor to arrive from Sam in Ballarat, fishing for rainbow trout in the creek, which we barbecued with dandelion roots.

Unfortunately, once installed, Patrick's new controller didn't last very long. The electric set-up we had was perfect for zipping around town, but carrying so much weight up steep hills obviously put too much strain on it. My electrics were also starting to play up. We called an e-bike shop in Sydney and booked our bikes in for a month's time. Patrick decided that he didn't want an electric motor on the tandem after all, but carrying so much weight and a heavy baby, I still felt I needed mine. Most long-distance cycle-tourers travel with anywhere from 20 to 50 kilograms of bike plus gear. I was travelling with nearly 80. At 158 centimetres and 50 kilos, my bike should have been a lot lighter, but we were travelling as a family and had no support vehicle shadowing us. A small motor to help me up the hills was a small sacrifice, though not everybody agreed.

'That's cheating!' was an accusation I heard from dozens of people when they saw I had a small motor in the hub of my front wheel.

'Is it?' I wondered aloud. 'Surely a car's cheating,' I would say, or 'Do you feel cheated?'

Having some assistance up the hills was also safer,

as without it, the weight made my bike increasingly unstable.

Before we left home, I thought that it would take longer to adjust to the rhythm of travelling, but each day we wriggled from our sleeping bags, we were open to the unavoidable possibility of everything. We were falling in love with our calendar-less life. We felt open in a way we didn't feel at home, perhaps because we no longer had our community and domestic responsibilities. We had cast ourselves adrift and, as a result, life was coming at us as we were coming at it.

In Tumut, the name derived from the Wiradjuri word meaning 'a quiet resting place by the river', we parked our bikes near the Tumut–Brungle Community Centre, where we were approached by some friendly men who wanted to know where we were headed. Patrick was then invited by one of them, local Aboriginal ranger Shane, to join the gathering of Wiradjuri men in their weekly men's honour workshop. While Woody and I explored a big box of handcrafted toys in the Centre, Patrick was introduced to the art of making traditional hunting tools, including fishing and roo spears and string made from stringybark, grasses and reeds.

The first year Patrick and I got together he started Just Free Water, a campaign that aimed to encourage people to boycott bottled water companies, particularly Coca-Cola Amatil, which had 70 per cent of the market, and whose Mount Franklin brand was the reason so much

On the road

of our water was sucked from the ground of our home region, paid virtually nothing for, packaged in plastic and trucked all over the country. Patrick wrote essays, had articles published in major newspapers, gave radio interviews and set up social-media stunts encouraging people to switch off Coke vending machines. So we were very excited, five weeks after leaving home, to be heading to Bundanoon in the Southern Highlands, Australia's first bottled-water-free town, not far from where he grew up. We arrived after a tedious several days' stretch on the Hume Highway in which we did little else but count thousands of slaughtered animals that had been hit by cars. In this time we made riverside camps in Gundagai, Jugiong, Yass and Gunning and in the evenings restored our battered senses by swimming, fishing and eating bulrush bulbs.

In Bundanoon, we met and stayed with Huw Kingston, who initiated the campaign that attracted international attention. Huw told us that on one day he did over 200 interviews with media agencies from around the world. He was part of a team that put together a set of guidelines for community groups and local councils to follow if they too wanted to rid their towns and cities of plastic water bottles. Because the Hume was fast and furious we were ahead of schedule again, and because of the friendly nature of the town we spent nearly a week in Bundanoon, staying with various people, and meeting our first fellow cycle-tourist, Jeff, an American on his fourth tour of Australia.

It was hard to leave Bundanoon. Every time we

found ourselves packed up and ready to move on, we met another person or family who invited us to stay, so when we really did have to go, we woke up extra early and crept out of town.

We were keen to get to Moss Vale, only 18 kilometres away, where we were met by Patrick's brother Sam, his wife Jacx and their two boys Freddy and Henry, who celebrated with us the 1000 kilometres we had ridden to get there. In the photo Sam took of us when we arrived, Patrick has his shirt off and is looking at the camera with a big, open and satisfied smile. Woody is looking around, wondering what all the commotion was that woke him, and there I am, pink in the face, shiny with sweat. My arms are raised, outstretched but exhausted, and I am radiant, over the moon, in a disbelieving, I-can't-believe-what-we-just-accomplished kind of way.

Or, more to the point, how-the hell-am-I-going-to-be-able-to-do-this-for-a-year?

Law-breakers

— Patrick —

MOSS VALE *to* COFFS HARBOUR
1000 KILOMETRES
22 *December* 2013 *to* 30 *March* 2014

At eight, I found a cigarette lighter and burnt down the timber shipping crate cubby I shared with my siblings. At thirteen I was picked up by the police for shooting protected birds with my air rifle in a public reserve. The next year, at three in the morning, I defecated on the local police sergeant's front porch and unknowingly dropped my wallet beside my steaming parcel in the process.

By the time the punk band Public Image Ltd entered my life, I had already accepted the naughty boy of the family role, the archetypal middle child. I hacked my hair, ripped my jeans, wagged school with friends, drank rocket fuel mixed from various spirits stolen from Dad's liquor cabinet. I was the private-school rebel cliché – privileged,

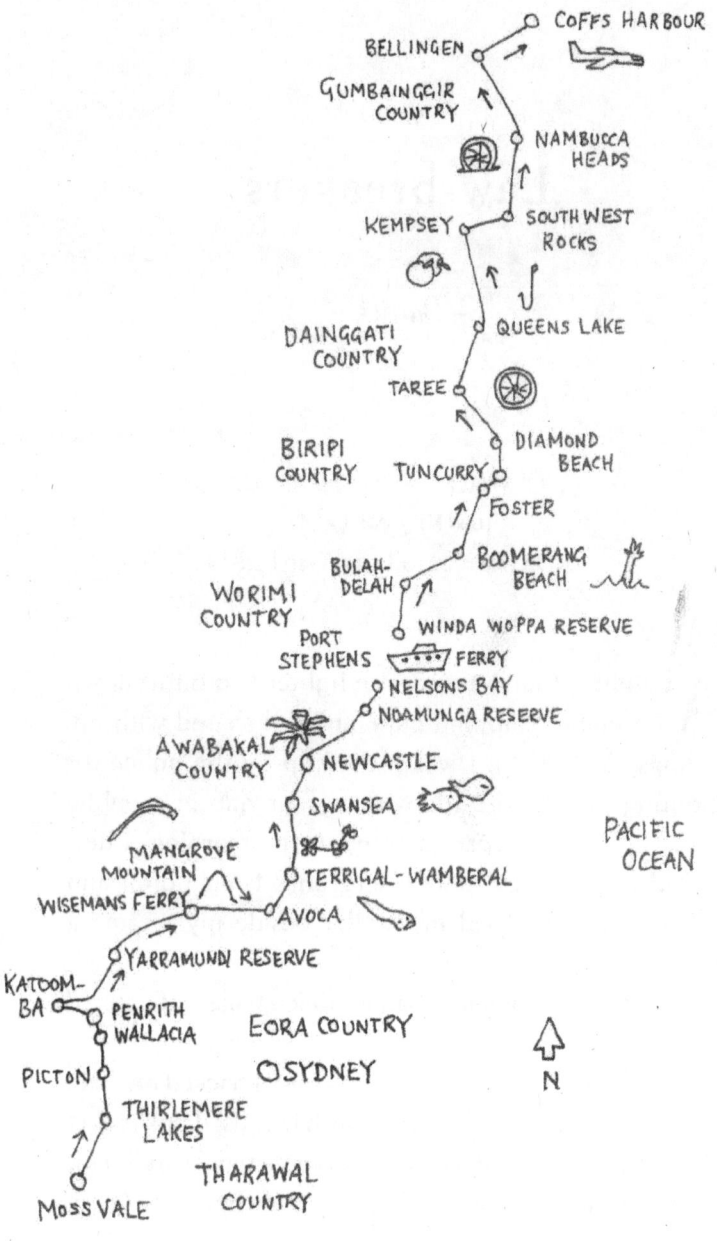

troubled and longing to front my own punk band. One night, when I was fifteen, I stuffed my bed with pillows, used a football as a replacement head and snuck out of the house. I met my friend Simon, who'd gotten hold of some vodka, and we downed the bottle in a nearby park. I came home half sober just before dawn, quietly put my bike under the house and tiptoed up the back stairs.

'WHERE THE HELL HAVE YOU BEEN?' boomed my father as I pushed open the back door.

My heart thumped so hard I thought it was going to explode. I'd snuck out countless times before, sometimes with my older brother and his friends to go roof-rocking or, if we found a patch, throw potatoes onto the roofs of unsuspecting town folk in the middle of the night. We were country kids and even sensible boys like my brother Sam couldn't resist the thrill of these stealthy escapades. But Sam would never have done anything as stupid as stuff his bed full of pillows and leave before Mum and Dad had returned from their party. He'd tried to stop me, but I had a rendezvous with my mate and mobile phones didn't exist in 1985.

'Breathe on me,' yelled Dad.

Oh shit, I'm in the biggest trouble.

'Breathe on me,' he demanded again.

I did as he asked and waited for the worst.

'Lucky you haven't had alcohol. Get to bed.'

Dad must have been so tired waiting up for me he'd lost his sense of smell. I was generally the kid holding the pin, even if I hadn't thrown the grenade. I was rarely this lucky.

I can appreciate what my parents went through with me. While I found them way too strict, they found me perennially unwilling to grow up. Returning to the Southern Highlands as a young adult was always unnerving and depressing. As I got older I found the old-guard conservatism of the region increasingly objectionable – economic entitlement, exclusive properties, English box hedges, ornamental pear trees. In my twenties I fantasised I was adopted, that one day I'd be told, and it would all make sense. In my thirties I wondered whether it was possible to cut all ties, while at the same time becoming increasingly interested in my forebears' working-class and peasant roots. But now in my forties I was determined to put all the nonsense to bed. I had travelled a thousand kilometres on bike with my gallant woman, our baby and our dog, and I was not going to let old scabs be knocked.

Zeph was supposed to come to Moss Vale with Mel's parents in their car en route to Sydney, but their Christmas plans changed at the last minute and there was no other choice but for Mel to put him on a plane. My sister Hen and her family, who live in Sydney, picked him up and drove him to Moss Vale and we were all reunited for a genuinely warm family Christmas.

All our bike seats were now full and Artist as Family – the name Meg and I gave our creative collective – felt like a complete tribe again. We stayed with Sam and his family for a week and with my parents for the same. My mother, Jan, writes articles for *Art Monthly* and shared with us films, books and artists she'd been saving to discuss. She was becoming interested in environmental art, and Dad, Robert, in semi-retirement from his various small businesses, was becoming more engaged with local sustainability groups in the district. As we were all ageing and I was perhaps mellowing, and some of our interests were aligning, our relationship seemed to be finally healing.

On a number of the evenings while we were in Moss Vale Zeph and I went rabbit-hunting with the timber longbow our friend Peter Yencken had made, which folded in two. Being collapsible meant our longbow tucked discreetly under Woody's bike seat, along with three arrows and a hand spear for fishing. Each night Zeph and I would dress in our darkest clothes and head out along the railway line east of the town.

'There's one, Dad,' Zeph tapped my arm and pointed.

We approached slowly and stalked to within 10 metres. As we'd planned Zeph clicked on our torch to stun the rabbit. My arrow shot through the night, but only produced a little puff of dust.

'You missed!' Zeph said, unimpressed.

It was by far our easiest chance. Still, we'd managed to get close to the rabbit and draw the string without it sensing us. I was pleased with that.

Zeph was born with one ear that can hear extremely well and one where the outer ear is closed over and can only hear vibrations. This biological reality had caused his behaviour to become fairly loose in a noisy classroom setting, missing instructions from teachers.

In quieter environments, where listening is more possible, Zeph's learning is palpable. However, in teaching him to stalk, one-on-one, I again realised how his mild to moderate deafness affects his way of being.

'Walk more quietly,' I whispered into his ear a dozen times on those nights.

'I am,' he'd whisper-yell back.

But the sticks and gravel and leaves crunching under his feet, and his excited impatience to see and set an arrow in the direction of a rabbit (as well as my poor aim), rendered our hunting expeditions no more than an enjoyable father-and-son experience. For Zeph this was Bear Grylls-ville; for me it was another attempt to develop our alternative economic model.

I was trying to teach Zeph what I was learning myself. To move as a predator requires moving with the knowledge of the wind, the ground, the night, the hunting tool and, most importantly, with knowledge of the prey itself. What I'd learnt so far was that to become a good hunter requires becoming more animal, and moving and thinking in our animal minds.

While I knew what I was doing in theory, aligning this knowledge in practice and not overthinking things was more difficult. Before my troubled teens my father taught me many useful things, such as how to propagate plants and keep chooks, but hunting wasn't one of them. Growing up, meat was something generally bought in a shop and, true to the times we lived in, there was no explanation about how that animal lived or died.

'Industrially farmed and transported food,' I lectured Zeph, as we walked home from another unsuccessful hunt, 'perpetuates the idea that humans are superior and have evolved to live in cities, and this is a big problem because if people can't see their resources – food, water, fuel, medicine, fibre – they don't really know what damage occurs in producing them. They've lost touch with these things.'

I sensed him rolling his eyes. Nevertheless he humoured me.

'But what happens when we catch nothing and we're really hungry?' Zeph asked.

It was a good question. Not that we were hungry; Mum had been keeping us all well fed.

'We eat cherry plums,' I said laughing.

Zeph was the only one in the AaF tribe who didn't find these weedy, abundant fruits delicious. While in Moss Vale we made numerous fruit leathers with cherry plums to take on our way. Things bought in bright wrappers and filled with refined sugar was more Zeph's thing, although his opportunities for such so-called food were few and far between.

'Humans are eating way too much meat,' I continued. 'While animal proteins evolutionarily grew our brains, especially when we started cooking them and we could capture all that incredible energy, eating so much animal protein today is turning the planet into a desert.'

'But I love meat, Dad.'

'And I love beer, but life is about limits. We live in

a culture that says limits don't exist and look what the result of that is. What sort of dad would I be if I just got drunk every day?'

'A pretty funny one?'

'Maybe, for a time. But after a while I'd become a grumpy dad, even more grumpy than I am usually.'

'That would be bad.'

'Oh, yes it would.'

Our first day's ride from Moss Vale was hot and dry. Zeph was excited to see for himself what cycle-touring was all about and what he learnt that day was the importance of conserving water. Because of our already heavy loads we could only carry 5 litres with us – not much for five mammals on two bikes. Keeping an eye out for water sources along the way was serious business. Each bike was carrying over 60 kilograms of gear. Including Zero, Zeph and I the tandem's total weight was 175 kilograms. On Meg and Woody's bike the total weight was 128 kilograms. As Meg's passenger didn't pedal and the weight of her motor and battery added 10 kilograms, she was working far harder on the flats than a regular cycle-tourer.

A week earlier we'd left Zero with my parents and their sweet dog Charles, put the bikes on the bus to Sydney, stayed with Hen and her family, got the electrics on Meg's bike sorted and removed the broken electrics from mine. The boys' Sydney cousins – Millie, Tildy and Eliza – were always a treat; Zeph excitedly swapped tween-culture notes, and Woody was doted on.

While in Sydney we also hosted a working bee at our *Food Forest*, a public artwork doubling as a community garden that we'd designed and installed in Surry Hills in 2010, commissioned by the Museum of Contemporary Art. We also visited *The Yeomans Project*, an exhibition by Ian Milliss and Lucas Ihlein at the Art Gallery of NSW. This exhibition celebrated the work of the Aussie farmer and plough-inventor, PA Yeomans, and recognised the junction at which the agricultural plough and 'culture' evidently meet. Both the plough and the fence are epic signals of settler intransigence in Australia, but Yeomans' plough at least allows the possibility of rehydration and nutrient-conserving of an otherwise ravaged country. Milliss and Ihlein's exhibition also showcased Australian artists who were working at the nexus of food and culture, including Artist as Family. We returned to Moss Vale spurred on by the public acknowledgement of our strange and mutable art practice.

This time, when we left the Southern Highlands, we bypassed Sydney. We cycled 52 kilometres from the ease of my parents' home back into the rough, and spent the night at Thirlmere Lakes National Park. We swam and waited for the sun to go down and the bushwalkers to drive off, and as we set up our tents the mosquitoes descended and we became their prey.

The logic of 'no dogs' in national parks is strange to us, and we felt justified in breaking whatever laws ruled Zero's illegitimacy. We buried his shit deep with ours and kept him on a lead. But the reason he was tethered was not to stop him chasing away the occasional bird but because the park was riddled with 1080 bait. We read the warning notices with disbelief. 1080 is still used in Australia for baiting foxes, dingoes, deer and other animals considered pests, but it's banned in almost all other countries because of how it spreads remorselessly through the food chain. Cars and 1080 were accepted in this 'nature' park, but NO dogs? I muzzled Zero's snout with my hand to stop him barking as we hid ourselves from a ranger who did a drive-by on dusk.

Another free meat that we sought to catch on this trip was common carp. Carp are considered an environmental menace in the cooler, willow-lined waterways throughout temperate Australia. So when we set up camp on the banks of the Nepean River near Wallacia a few days later and set about fishing for bass with surface lures, we very unexpectedly and unconventionally landed a good-sized, bottom-feeding carp. The local boy who actually caught the fish was about to throw it back (after having his photo taken holding it) when Zeph asked him whether we could have it. I knew it would be good eating, despite the bad press the fish has among Aussies. I'd heard Australians of Chinese and Eastern European descent speak highly of carp as they fished for them in Lake Daylesford. After a little research that night I found out that carp had to be eaten straightaway or put on ice because, as the animal's body temperature rises, it releases histamines that give the meat a muddy flavour. We did neither of these things, and instead hung the fish in nightshade while we slept, and cooked it for breakfast the following day.

All the misconceptions about this now common feral fish dissolved with each mouthful. There was no muddiness despite the Nepean being a heavily disturbed river with motorboats, conventional agriculture and storm-water damage, and despite the long period of time the animal was out of the water.

'People just aren't hungry enough,' said Meg.

Carp was enthusiastically added to our growing list of free tucker.

After a few days on the Nepean we left our river camp of muddy swimming and fishy treats and headed to Penrith in heatwave conditions. Because of the forecasted 40-degree day and the steep climb ahead we hid Zero in a wine box that sat snugly in his bike basket and took a train from Penrith to Blackheath, a thousand metres above sea level.

After alighting, we gravity-fed ourselves down from the station, rolling through the streets of the upper Blue Mountains searching for a campsite. We spent a hot afternoon in Katoomba continuing our search and, on nearing dusk, a little desperate, we approached a man in a park who we thought might be local to ask if he could recommend a place. Shane, who'd lost his legs in a work accident, hopped on his quad bike and invited us to follow him. He lead us to a quiet little bush site, a ten-minute walk to the heart of town and a two-minute amble to a hidden billabong. It was at this camp, on our third day, that we received our first visit from the police.

The afternoon before, I was pushing back the undergrowth that hid our tents, about to go and fill up the water bottles when I was startled by a bushwalker. Or rather, he was startled by me. As our eyes registered I became aware that Woody was crying in the tent nearby, Meg struggling to get him down for his afternoon sleep. The man looked horrified and I must have looked guilty. This was made worse when he didn't return my smile and 'G'day,' but instead scurried off in a kind of panic.

Great, I thought, he's going to run to the nearest ranger and dob us in for camping here. But no one came that evening and we went to bed thinking that the guy was just a little nervy and antisocial and thought nothing more of it.

The next morning Meg and I woke to the sound of a line of cars coming down the little cul de sac near our camp that no one had driven down since we moved in.

'What the hell's going on here, sounds like an army,' I muttered, slipping on my jeans as we heard car doors open and close. I crawled out of the tent.

'It's the police,' I passed on to Meg.

I was pretty anxious by the roll-up and could see several officers coming through the bush from different tracks. Don't worry, guys, I thought to myself as they drew closer, I'm not going to do a runner. I don't believe what we're doing is such a big deal.

'G'day, are we not supposed to camp here?' I said as jovially as I could.

The first man on the scene wasn't in uniform but

smartly dressed and seemed to be in charge of this exorbitant mission. He replied surprised but encouragingly, 'No, I think you're OK to camp here.'

He asked to see my licence. I was racking my mind to think what we'd published on our blog of late that might have raised the ire of the authorities. As the check was carried out on my licence I sensed that these cops were actually federal police – surely local cops would have come the previous night if they'd been alerted to our presence by the bushwalker.

The licence check was taking some time, which caused me to wonder if they'd found a linked file to my ID that documented my 'Deserter Memorial #4', a temporary, portable, bright red anti-war cenotaph I had built and later installed outside Kirribilli House in 2002. At the time Prime Minister John Howard was talking up Australia's involvement in bombing the hell out of Iraq on the hypocritical grounds of Iraq having weapons of mass destruction. I was later visited by three members of the federal police in my Trentham bookshop, and questioned. Not much happened, apart from low to moderate levels of paranoia on my part for a few months afterwards.

The licence came back, they thanked me for my time and proceeded to leave.

'Hey, why are we being investigated?' I asked the main guy.

'Your camp fitted the description of some people who have gone missing. There's a nationwide search going on,' he said.

Later we came across the news story. Two weeks after our stop in the Blue Mountains the bodies of a father and his young daughter were found in sandhills near Pottsville in northern NSW. The bushwalker had obviously been following the story. The horror on his face on seeing me and hearing Woody cry now seemed justified.

Meg turned 40 in Katoomba and we were joined by her parents to celebrate. Ross and Vivienne had come by plane, bus and train from Daylesford, where they'd recently moved to be closer to their five grandchildren, which, from the beginning, lovingly included Zeph. On the door of their motel room on the morning we arrived for the birthday breakfast, Ross and Vivienne had pinned a handmade poster comprising photographs of Meg's progression from baby to adult, a long-standing Ulman tradition.

We all took the opportunity to wash before we went out.

'Ah, a warm shower,' Meg sighed, gleaming with washed hair in a light summer op-shopped dress. I loved how little she concerned herself with her appearance. It wasn't unimportant, just a low priority. She observed her greying hair and ageing body and welcomed them both, which only made me love her more.

In Katoomba we collected the bright orange flowerbuds of common daylillies that had naturalised in the park where we'd met Shane, and cooked them up as part of a meal we made in exchange for staying with a local family who rescued us from the rain. In gratitude I also did a permaculture design for their garden.

We rolled down to Leura and stayed with eco-poet friends, Kate Fagan and Peter Minter, and their gorgeous young children Ruby and Felix. Kate had so thoroughly, intelligently and lovingly supervised my thesis. We rode on and caught fish and camped a week at Yarramundi, where we met the Wheelers, a home-ed family who invited us to spend a night at their home in Wilberforce. We meandered north from there along the Hawkesbury River, crossed it at Wisemans Ferry and happened upon the notorious bikie and former jailed 'supreme commander' of the Comancheros, William George 'Jock' Ross, at a working bee where he was the captain, in charge of the Spencer Rural Fire Service. He kindly let Meg recharge her bike battery. Not far on we caught two short-finned eels at Mangrove Creek and with these fierce animals in our breakfast bellies climbed the 5-kilometre ascent up Mangrove Mountain where Zeph showed us his incredible rigour.

'A hill is just a hill, Dad,' he said confidently, as I lay wasted on a grassy verge at the top of the range, where we ate lunch and gathered up the strength to push on.

We stayed with a family in Erina Heights (who contacted us through our blog) and a family in Avoca (who Meg begged to take us in when we were caught out in a heavy storm), then stealth-camped, spear-fished, ate bower spinach and enjoyed watching Zeph build a thatched cubby out of she-oak needles in our hidey-hole spot beside the Wamberal lagoon just north of Terrigal. It was our first coastal camp.

We stayed a week in this forest of she-oaks and paperbarks, wedged between the Pacific Ocean and high-density suburbia. During the day we'd walk or ride the few kilometres south to Terrigal and Zeph and I would snorkel around the rocks at the southern end of the beach with our hand spear at the ready. The first ocean fish we caught was a lovely dusky flathead just off the rocks. I speared it and hurled it to Zeph to gut and protect from the persistent, scavenging seagulls. Meg and Woody played on the beach or slept for a while in the park, where we would cook our catches on the public barbecues.

While in Wamberal we contacted and were offered hot water and meals by our first Warm Showers hosts, Rod and Deb. Warm Showers is an international couch-surfing website for cycle-tourers; we are hosts back home. The idea is when hungry, stinky cyclists pedal through your neck of the woods they are welcomed, fed and provided with a towel. It's yet another gift economy that the internet has helped create.

Just north of The Entrance, we chanced upon and camped with fellow cycle-tourer Tom, a recent engineering graduate from Melbourne. We immediately liked this footloose dude and Zeph was as enamoured by his hammock tent as his Ned Kelly beard.

'When I grow up I'm going to travel Australia by bike with a tent like that,' he said after Tom left the next morning. I was waiting for him to add beard.

'You're basically doing that now, Zeph,' Meg laughed, folding up Woody's clothes.

'Yeah, but on my own, or with a friend.'

We understood. His little brother still wasn't big enough for him to play with and his parents weren't really meeting his social needs.

We ate warrigal greens in Swansea. We spent three weeks in Newcastle eating street-lined lilly pillies, spearing blackfish and sand whiting, collecting pigface fruits, staying with a host of families, Zeph attending the local Steiner school, and sneak-camping on Awabakal country near the Glenrock Lagoon where I speared a bagful of yellowfin bream.

While cooking the fish in olive oil and garlic we threw in the young leaves of pigface to cook in the juices. Cooked this way and with a drizzle of lemon, the astringency of the leaves disappeared and was great tucker.

We would try this recipe again at Gerry Bobsien's home several days later, though not with the same success. Gerry, a friend, author, and champion of AaF, had invited me to do an artist-in-residency in Newcastle in 2009 when she was the director of the Lock-up Cultural Centre. From that invitation Meg and I established Artist as Family, and proposed an alternative residency – a 17-day family holiday that then seven-year-old Zeph, Meg and I would spend foraging for anthropogenic waste along the coastline and throughout the city. Gerry greenlighted our proposal. We amassed an enormous pile of food and drink packaging, which we walked or biked back to the Centre in bags and backpacks. The work took the form of a 1-metre wide, 20-metre long line of non-disposable rubbish exhibited in the old prison exercise yard, the plastics of which we'd stopped from becoming part of the great Pacific garbage patch. We blogged our experience each day – the people we met, our discoveries about plastics and their unhappy incursion on marine life, and the final horrifying pile.

Zeph turned twelve in Newcastle and we took him to his first big concert – Macklemore and Ryan Lewis, who just happened to be in the city for a one-off gig on his actual birthday. Woody and Zero stayed with Fiona and Phil, Kiwi baby-boomers on working visas who, like Gerry, really looked out for us out while we were in this city. The concert was a spectacle of gigantic proportions; the lighting alone would have powered a small Pacific island for several weeks. Zeph loved it and Macklemore's charisma fixed itself into his boy-brain psyche like first big concerts do. (Mine was Queen; Meg's was George Michael.)

We left Newcastle by the Stockton Ferry, which we were told was Australia's shortest ferry ride. It took all of seven minutes but saved us hours of travelling in busy traffic around the city. Zero was for once legitimate and didn't require hiding. He did, however, require a muzzle to board. We'd earlier made a makeshift one with cardboard and gaffer tape.

We soon began a very hot day's ride along the loud and furious Nelson Bay Road to Noamunga Reserve. We all stripped off for a swim in the ocean and pitched

Law-breakers

our tents, much to the disdain of a local man who took exception to Zeph rabbiting with the longbow in the public reserve across the road from his home.

'They're lookin' at me, comin' towards me,' he shouted into his mobile.

Yes, I was looking at him up on his balcony as he hurriedly ushered his small daughters inside the enormous fortress of a house, and I did start to walk towards him to say, 'Hey, I'm just a dad trying to teach my son how to bag one of these plentiful mammals for dinner.'

When his panic escalated I turned around and walked away. We set up our tents in the 'no camping, no dogs' reserve, cooked a peasant's pasta (*sans* rabbit) and waited for our second visit from the police.

Two policemen showed up about 40 minutes later. One raised the issue of taking up residence in a no camping, no dog area. 'People pay rates, you can see how they'd get annoyed by freeloaders.'

Freeloaders!

'You should check in with the local council in the morning and ask them for permission to camp here,' said the second policeman. 'I can see you are with children, so stay here tonight.'

His kindness shifted things. We were so caught up in the intention of our trip – living on and feeding ourselves from what was left of public land – that we'd become lax in our decision-making. The police could see that Zeph and his weapon were not a real threat to anyone and they left us in peace.

I was tired and the ocean looked cold and rough, but I was determined to catch dinner that night. It was about a week since our latest encounter with the police. We were at Boomerang Beach, about 150 kilometres north, after a hard day's riding from Bulahdelah. I asked Zeph to scout for me as I jumped in near the rocks that formed the base of the point, spear in hand and snorkelling gear on. Almost immediately I was caught in a rip and ferociously sucked out. I put up my hand to signal to Zeph I needed help and saw him run off in Meg's direction, who was with Woody and Zero about half a kilometre away.

'Shit!' I shouted out. 'The nearest adult!'

As I watched Zeph climb the steps that led over the sand dunes I got severe cramps in both my calf muscles, no doubt from all the hill-climbing we'd done that day, dehydration, and now kicking furiously with burly flippers.

I struggled to tread water. The rip had initially run parallel to the outcrop of rocks but was beginning to arch away from them, taking me with it. I tried to stretch out, then relax my painful calves, but as soon as I stopped using my flippers I sank, swallowing a mouthful of seawater. I don't know why I held onto my spear because I had to use all my upper body strength to keep afloat. I kept sinking and taking in water, cramping and thrashing my arms to get my head up for air, until fate intervened. A big wave coming in from a colliding current crashed over me from behind. I came up gasping for air, panicking.

'Fuck,' I screamed spluttering water.

The sea thrummed indifferently. But the wave had released me from the rip. Another wave followed, moving me rapidly to the ocean end of the rock platform. A third wave drove me onto a concealed rock ledge on which I stood and hurled my spear to higher ground. I clambered onto another ledge and, holding on with one hand, tried to get my cumbersome flippers off when a fourth wave belted me. I felt the skin of my right shoulder tear on rock. I grabbed whatever hard surface I could as the force of the wave sucked back out. I quickly worked to get both my flippers off and jumped higher again as another wave belted in. I could see Meg holding Woody to her hip, running with Zeph and Zero along the back of the rock platform. They were screaming at me. I made my way to my spear, collected it, noticing the bent and blunted prongs, and started hobbling on bleeding feet towards my family, crying.

Meg was irate, and repeatedly hitting my arm.

'You're a bloody idiot, Jonesy!' she screamed.

Zeph was assessing the cuts on my shoulder. 'Looks bad, Dad.'

Meg took a look, and started crying and kissing me all over my back.

I didn't care that I could hardly walk and my shoulder was pounding. All I knew was that somehow I wasn't white and limp, breathless and sharkmeat.

In my desperation to tell another story, enact another way to live, I'd failed to observe the laws of the natural world. I had put ideology before safety. Was that what I was doing with this whole adventure? It wasn't only my own safety I was risking but my family's, riding these violent and dangerous roads and sleeping rough to make a point about pollution and damage, mass war and unjustness. While *Free Tucker* was our positive motivation, we had also been sharing on our blog the thousands of kilometres of roadkill and plastic food-and-drink packaging we encountered along the way. It didn't exactly make us hopeful that solar-powered cars and biodegradable wrapping materials would end the normalised brutality of contemporary life.

We bought pizza for dinner that night. I stopped myself from thinking about the chemicals in the ingredients, and about the toxic phthalates or plasticisers that were more than likely in the cardboard box, sweating into and permeating our so-called food. I even blocked out the annihilated forests that produced the biodegradable packaging, and simply enjoyed the pizza with my family on a little timber platform overlooking rugged Boomerang Beach.

That night we all collapsed in our protected hideout in the paperbark forest, under the spell of the ocean's unrelenting whir. Before we slept Meg and I talked. Even though I'd nearly drowned that afternoon we never entertained we'd end our trip.

Life involves death. We both understood this. Being killed riding these roads and trying to procure food for my family was, for me, preferable to staying at home, fearing the world. If something happened to Meg or me while trying to perform a transition from what Australian writer Deborah Bird Rose calls 'man-made mass death' to environmental accountability, then that was our fate. We were fully committed to this trip. But if anything happened to our boys – that was an entirely different story.

A gentle flat morning's ride brought us to the senior-citizen-filled city of Forster, where we hung out at the public library, putting Woody to sleep on some large cushions under a desk. Zeph watched a movie while Meg and I blogged. While I was out the front of the library making sure Zero had enough shade and water I got talking to Glenn, a fellow cyclist, who was eager to hear our story. He invited us to spend the night at his home with his family. It turned out Glenn was the General Manager of the Forster–Tuncurry City Council.

The next day we rode through the town centre and crossed the remarkably long Forster–Tuncurry Bridge in search of a place to camp. We swam, line-fished and cooked up our catch on a free public barbecue before setting up the tents well after dark, hidden behind some bushes near the Tuncurry Rock Pool. We were all sleeping soundly until around 1 am when Meg and I were woken to spritzes of water hitting our face.

'What the hell?' I lashed.

We quickly realised that a brigade of pop-up sprinklers had been timed to come on automatically. The angle they were set at meant their rotating jets could fire straight through our tent's air vents, soaking us and our bedding. For the next hour, Meg and I took it in turns holding one particular jet away from our camp. The previous night we had been wined and dined by the GM in a plush home, the next night we were illegitimates in a public park, soaked in our undies, laughing at my silliness at having chosen such green grass to bed down on, without thinking how it got to be so lush on the world's driest inhabited continent.

It was also my mistake that the front wheel of the tandem became severely buckled the next day. We arrived at Red Head, just 20 kilometres north of Tuncurry, and found bike racks outside a holiday resort to park our heavy two-wheeled caravans. We went into the office to ask for a free map of the area and when we came out there was the tandem, all 60-plus kilos of it, set at 30 degrees off the ground except for the front wheel, which was obediently waiting in the rack where I'd parked it. I managed to straighten the wheel enough to ride to the end of the road where we found a little hidden reserve and pitched our tents for a few days. I just didn't have the energy to deal with it.

A pop-up sprinkler disturbing my sleep was rare; it was more often Woody or Zeph calling out in their sleep, or Zero barking at a possum sniffing around our food pannier. Once woken it would sometimes take me hours to get back to sleep. Before I became a father, an older man told me that his sleep changed forever when he became a dad. I had no idea then what he meant. I now do.

Law-breakers

The nights I slept well meant the day that unfurled would be easy, and I was better equipped for any challenge thrown my way. But the days that followed broken sleep would see me go into a grumpy shell. Perhaps it was my due, sent from the roof-rocking karma god, but these extreme oscillations in my mental state made me recognise the profound medicine of sleep.

On the morning we were ready to push off from our little coastal nook we thought the best thing to do was to get the bikes to nearby Black Head, from where I would catch a bus to Taree with the wheel and get the rim properly straightened. When we got to Black Head, David, a local resident wandered up to us, fascinated to see another tandem just like his own, which he had purchased with his 80-year-old neighbour Walter for their weekly outings.

We had the good fortune to go back to David's home and meet his two girls Isabel and Lucy. They shared delicious eggs from their Isa Brown chooks, and we stayed in a little garden bungalow that David built from reclaimed materials. We had just unpacked and set up the beds when a serious windstorm crashed through the district, bringing down trees and powerlines. The next day David took the wheel with him to work in Taree and got it fixed at his local bike shop.

The 120-kilometre stretch along the Pacific Highway between Taree and Kempsey was stressful, with long sections of road that had little or no shoulder, and a constant stream of cars and trucks. It was brutal. I know well what it's like to be inside the bubble of a car – it doesn't feel all that violent. But on a bicycle the abuse materialises as an endless stream of aggression. The repeating stench of morbidity and deafening carelessness was an all-out assault on our senses.

We camped unlawfully again on a forested bank of the beautiful Queens Lake, and rose with the sun to ride to Kempsey to meet an old friend from Daylesford. It was to be our longest day of riding so far, 83 kilometres, and we joyously collapsed at Brett's family home, worn out and relieved for some respite.

Brett was recuperating in Kempsey too. He was just back from doing aid work in Lebanon with Médecins Sans Frontières, and staying with his brother in what was formerly their grandparents' home. When Brett lived in Daylesford we did loads of great stuff together, including getting the Daylesford Community Food Gardens up and growing, and bicycle advocacy group Critical Mass Daylesford up and cycling. We also formed a band, A Bunch of Bandits, with two other close friends, Fe and Ant. We were a happy folk-punk rabble, and I finally got to be a contemptuous, out-of-key frontman singing ridiculous lyrics ripped and collaged from politically incorrect comics from the 1980s.

We had three days with Brett and Kurt. I spent long sessions in bed before we set out. We would see Brett again a little further north, and he mapped out for us a quiet route that meandered along the Macleay River to the pretty coastal town of South West Rocks, where we rode around till dusk looking for a discreet home for the night. In desperation, only after the last of the evening walkers had disappeared, we pitched our tents on a fairly conspicuous walking path near the beach.

By now pitching the tents and making up the beds took around fifteen minutes. Zeph was in charge of setting up the boys' tent, and while Meg breastfed Woody to sleep, Zeph and I would talk or read our books in the adults' tent.

The next morning, we were woken by Zero barking at early-morning walkers. We packed up, made porridge on our gas stove and took to the road again. It was only after lunch, after we'd followed the other side of the Macleay River out to rejoin the terrifying Pacific Highway, that the tandem had what was to be our very first puncture, about 1800 kilometres into the trip. We made lunch, I patched the tube, refitted the tyre and then cursed and ranted like a fitful child when I realised I put the tyre on the wrong rotation. It was just a little thing, but I was really worn out – I never thought I'd ever again feel rested – and we were now on a deadline to get to Coffs Harbour by the end of March where Zeph would leave us. I thought back to Nick's comment about the times that we'll want to find a shed for the bikes and put them away for a few weeks. But we had to keep moving.

I refitted the tyre and we rode to Nambucca Heads, only to get another puncture in the same tube on arrival. Although we didn't recognise it at the time, our tyres were wearing through. With our late arrival and threatening storm clouds brewing we booked into our first motel. We had been living on about $35 a day; a $100 motel room was budget-breaking, to say the least. After some gentle persuasion the owners allowed us to have Zero in the room. The heavens opened as I fixed the tube in the bath, locating the tiny hole by the bubbling air under the water. Meg and I made dinner, washed clothes and bodies and later, when the boys were asleep, gave motel-room sex a burl.

Zeph particularly loved this brief moment of civil reprieve. With his arms folded behind his head, wrapped in a bleached white towel after a stint in the chlorinated pool, he watched and watched TV until he passed out.

There was a distinct humid grassy smell that was becoming increasingly common the more north we got; it smelt like fermenting cannabis. It was around here, in the mid-north of the New South Wales coast, that Meg, Woody and I fell in love with guavas. Zeph and Zero – the Zeds, as Meg had named these two – fully rejected them. Guavas, being tenacious self-proliferators, had naturalised along the coast since at least Kempsey, where we first spotted them. When we arrived in Bellingen, the fruit was in abundance, but then again everything was; it was so lush and fertile, it seemed you could grow anything. When we left this little utopian town, thinking how we might possibly arrange to live there after communing with a number of good folk and families over three days, we stocked up on locally grown organic produce and rode our laden bikes along the quiet gravel backroads north to Coffs Harbour.

Zeph's first three months with us were now over.

'You've ridden from Moss Vale to Coffs Harbour,' I praised him at the airport. 'That's at least a thousand kilometres!'

Being twelve, he was old enough to travel unaccompanied to Melbourne, where he'd be collected by his adoring mum who'd cook him all the food he loves and pay him undivided attention. Zeph had been missing her madly and as he counted down the days to leaving us his excitement turned into rebellion. It didn't help that his father had been struggling with tiredness and was always trying to get him to taste new things. While at first Zeph engaged whole-heartedly with our intentions for the trip, after a thousand kilometres, he'd begun to resent them.

Meg and I had been bickering more and more as Zeph's departure day drew closer, mostly about how best to parent him in his current mood. We were also becoming increasingly depressed that we were putting him on a plane again. It mocked the very point of our trip.

It would be six months before we saw Zeph again, by far the longest we'd be apart. He walked so confidently across the tarmac, not looking back once and ascended the stairs to the rear of the plane.

'Goodbye, Zeph,' I mumbled pathetically as I watched the craft take off from behind giant panels of plate glass.

Meg and I were crying. Woody was confused and kept asking, 'Where 'ephyr? Where 'ephyr?'

'He's gone to Aunty Mel's,' we repeated again and again over the next several days.

'Aunty Mel n 'ephyr in sky?' he'd ask with as much regularity. Every time he saw a plane he'd ask whether it was them.

We walked outside the airport terminal to where Zero was waiting with the bikes, unlocked them from underneath the 'No Bicycles' sign, and rode away from that painful place.

Embracing uncertainty

– Meg –

COFFS HARBOUR to BENTLEY
300 KILOMETRES
30 March 2014 to 17 April 2014

At home I sometimes cried when Zeph went off to Mel's for her half-week – three-and-a-half days seemed like an eternity. How would we go without seeing him for six whole months? We would miss him, ache for him, and talk about him all the time, but his leaving also made things much simpler – we no longer had a pre-teen hurricane in our midst.

Zephyr was four when I came along. He wasn't in nappies and was old enough to feed and dress himself. He already had a mother, and didn't really need me to play that role, but there I was anyway, preparing the foods he liked, washing his clothes, planning his birthday parties, dressing up as a pirate and sailing the high seas with him on the ship of our upturned kitchen table.

The Art of Free Travel

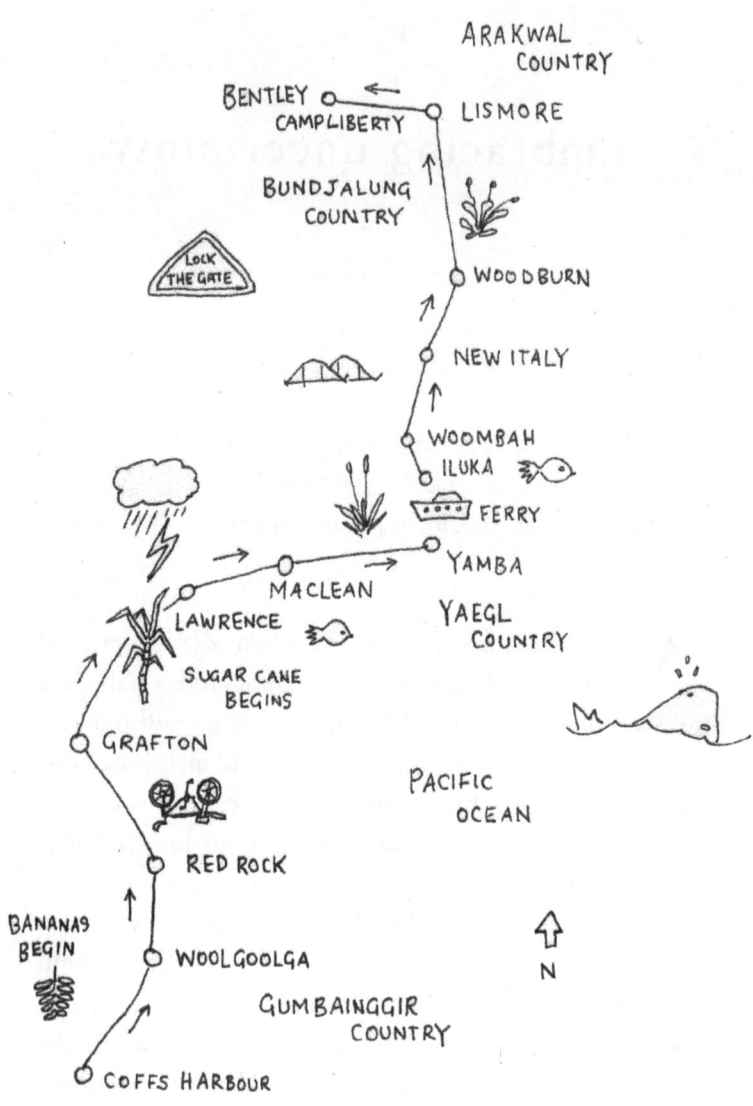

Embracing uncertainty

I was a maternal figure, but not a mother.

When we started calling ourselves Artist as Family, it satisfied in me something very deep. We chose the name as a response to the individualism of western art, and to show how we operated more as a creative tribe. It seemed to embrace all my inferiorities. It seemed to swallow up and accept that awkward prefix step-, while so easily embosoming all the positive things I felt I brought to our little clan. There was room for all of us.

When we farewelled Zeph, we all felt a little lost. Woody kept asking after his brother, and Patrick and I felt as I imagine empty-nesters might feel when their kids leave home. Our boy didn't need us. He had hugged us farewell then walked stoically onto the plane without a final glimpse or wave. I had felt so proud of him. He seemed so grown up, a young man making his own way in the world.

But I also felt hurt as he reeled off the list of all the things he was most looking forward to about being home with this mum. 'She has a car so I don't have to ride my bike everywhere, she shops at the supermarket and let's me eat whatever I want, she buys me treats, she cooks me meat every night for dinner, she lets me play games on her phone.'

Even though I knew not all of these things were true, I understood their appeal to him, that he was caught between two homes and their differences.

In Coffs Harbour we were approached by Mark and Denise, two avid cyclists, who invited us to stay with them in Woolgoolga. We rode the 25 kilometres to their home, noticing as we entered the township a striking white double-storey structure with arches, extensive balcony and bell tower turret guarded by two statues of men in traditional garb atop white horses. It was the Guru Nanak Sikh Temple, the town's main architectural attraction in one of Australia's largest Sikh communities.

In Mark and Denise's backyard there was a five-metre-high metal frame on which Denise suspended long lengths of silk, from which she wrapped, hung, fell and swung. It was part-ballet and part-circus acrobatics, but looked like she was doing it all underwater. Her impromptu performances showed off her great strength and poise, and four-and-a-half months after we left home, I felt a first pang of homesickness. Denise reminded me of our friend Mara, who teaches circus skills. Before we planned our trip, I had been looking forward to taking Woody to her classes and watching him develop his strength and agility alongside his little friends.

Mark, who plays the tin whistle, also performed for us. I play the tin whistle in our band, and had one in my handlebar bag, always at the ready though I rarely played it. Whenever I had the inclination, we were camping somewhere illegitimately and I feared attracting unwanted attention. Mark's playing made me miss home too. I started longing for afternoons with Fe and Ant, imagining our kids, who were crawling when we left, dancing and singing along as we jammed.

Above Arriving in Moss Vale, New South Wales, after our first 1000 kilometres, greeted by Aunty Jackie and Cousin Freddy. Photo taken by Uncle Sam. Early summer 2013.
Below Picking roadside apples in the Blue Mountains, New South Wales. Midsummer 2014.

Above Preparing dinner at our campsite at Yarramundi, New South Wales. Midsummer 2014.
Below Zephyr in his she-oak cubby at Wamberal Lagoon, New South Wales. Late summer 2014.

Above Another flat tyre as we approach Grafton, New South Wales. Mid-autumn 2014.
Below Farewelling Gate A with fellow protector Kai Wild. Bentley Blockade, northern New South Wales. Late autumn 2014.

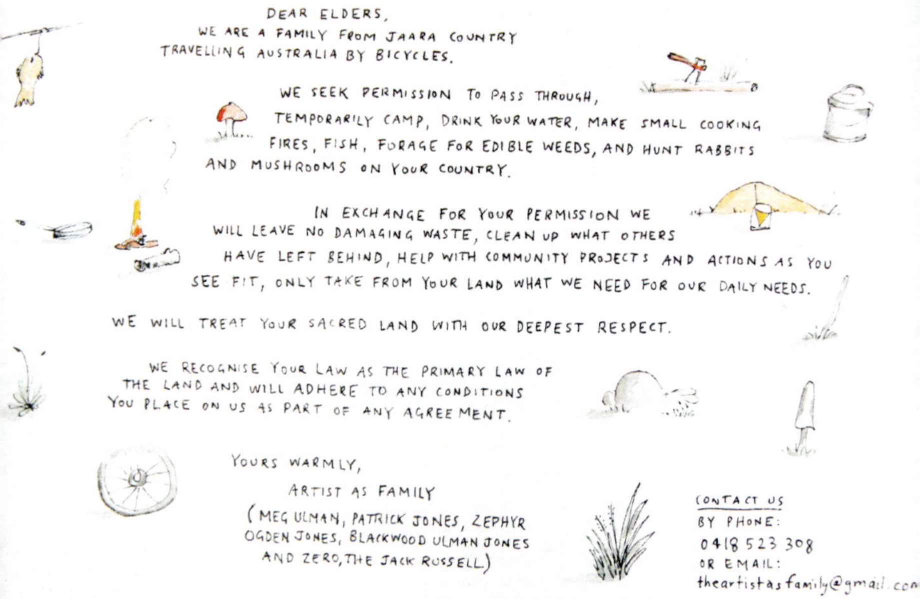

DEAR ELDERS,
WE ARE A FAMILY FROM JAARA COUNTRY
TRAVELLING AUSTRALIA BY BICYCLES.

WE SEEK PERMISSION TO PASS THROUGH,
TEMPORARILY CAMP, DRINK YOUR WATER, MAKE SMALL COOKING
FIRES, FISH, FORAGE FOR EDIBLE WEEDS, AND HUNT RABBITS
AND MUSHROOMS ON YOUR COUNTRY.

IN EXCHANGE FOR YOUR PERMISSION WE
WILL LEAVE NO DAMAGING WASTE, CLEAN UP WHAT OTHERS
HAVE LEFT BEHIND, HELP WITH COMMUNITY PROJECTS AND ACTIONS AS YOU
SEE FIT, ONLY TAKE FROM YOUR LAND WHAT WE NEED FOR OUR DAILY NEEDS.

WE WILL TREAT YOUR SACRED LAND WITH OUR DEEPEST RESPECT.

WE RECOGNISE YOUR LAW AS THE PRIMARY LAW OF
THE LAND AND WILL ADHERE TO ANY CONDITIONS
YOU PLACE ON US AS PART OF ANY AGREEMENT.

YOURS WARMLY,
ARTIST AS FAMILY
(MEG ULMAN, PATRICK JONES, ZEPHYR
OGDEN JONES, BLACKWOOD ULMAN JONES
AND ZERO, THE JACK RUSSELL)

CONTACT US
BY PHONE:
0418 523 308
OR EMAIL:
theartistasfamily@gmail.com

Above Our *Letter to elders*, drawn by Patrick in Mullumbimby, northern New South Wales. Late autumn 2014.
Below Not quite two years old and Woody is eager to contribute, Calliope River, south-central Queensland. Winter 2014.

Above Running out of water on the 120 kilometre gravel Ridgelands–Glenroy Station Road, central Queensland. Dry season 2014.
Below Meg and Woody meeting Ashley Boyd on Palm Island, Far North Queensland. Dry season 2014.

Above Zaymon McGreen holds hands with Woody as we ride into Hope Vale, East Cape York. Dry season 2014.
Below Our last night with Guugu Yimithirr elders, Elaine and Tim McGreen (seated) and family members (from left) Bryanne, Christine, Ricky and Deltone in Hope Vale, East Cape York. Dry season 2014.

Above Patrick hand-spears another delicious red morwong in Mollymook, New South Wales. Late spring 2014.
Below Patrick gutting a road-killed possum at our camp, Cann River, north-east Victoria. Early summer 2014.

Above Zeph takes a break on the tandem near Pambula, south-east New South Wales. Early summer 2014.
Below Setting up camp on our second last night, Beckingsale Bushland Reserve, Central Victoria. Midsummer 2015.

Music had always been a big part of our homelife, and it was no different on the road. People often asked how Woody handled sitting on the back of my bike for hours at a time. Since the day he was born he was chilled out. Whereas Zeph experiences the world physically, Woody has always been happy to sit and observe, to watch how things are done before attempting them himself. Where Woody would stand before a tree to take it all in, asking what kind it was and whether its fruit were edible, Zephyr's first concern would be the quickest way to scale it. Woody's innately placid nature meant he was happy to just sit on the back of the bike, but music certainly made things more enjoyable.

Every day, everything we saw and experienced got turned into a song that I would sing to him over and over. It was like living inside a musical. There was, among our repertoire, the uphill song, the downhill song, the bridge song, the truck song, the roadkill song, the seedpod song, the caravan song, the bike song, the bike-shop song, the song about the possum that ate our breakfast, the unsealed road song, the beach song, the grazing animal song, and later, about 100 kilometres north of Woolgoolga in Lawrence, where we first saw sugarcane growing, all the way to far north Queensland, we sang the sugarcane song. Some of the songs were only a few lines long and some, like the caravan song, grew the more grey nomads we met, until it was nearly 20 verses long.

Sometimes Patrick would sing to us little jingly tunes of his own.

'It's great,' I would tease, 'it just needs a little more work. Get back to me in 200 kilometres.'

'Riding 70 kilometres is easy!' I laughed to Patrick at the end of one particularly long day. 'Try riding while singing songs. The. Entire. Time. Now *that's* a challenge!'

The more we talked and sang, the more engaged Woody became, and the more he enjoyed spending time on the bike.

While music helped make the lengthy stretches of road more interesting for Woody, his dexterity did too. Where once I had to stop riding to give him a drink of water from one of the three bottles on our bike, by eighteen months he was able to grab the bottle I passed back to him while we were still moving. Before we attempted this manoeuvre with a bottle, we had lots of practice with loquats and pieces of apple or almonds, many of which he dropped, but he never let a bottle fall.

When we were camping we let him play with the hatchet and our pocketknives, carefully observing his play and teaching him about their sharpness. We'd read that Inuit babies are exposed to sharp knives and soon develop a respect and care for them as they learn from adults how to carefully peel the flesh of fish from blades. We watched the same development with Woody.

The more time we spent living on the ground, the more Woody thrived. Indoors, raised above the earth, there are rules and walls and edges. Outside, the world is expansive. Everything is relational. You see the ants on their nest? That's why we can't camp over here because we don't want to disturb them.

Inside there are lightbulbs that keep us separate from our diurnal circadian rhythms, meaning we don't go to sleep when the sun does, despite how hard we try to get to bed early.

Before Woody was born we decided that he wouldn't have any toys. We didn't want plastic landfill cluttering our living space. We even felt that educational wooden toys were too prescriptive. We let our families and friends know, and quietly gave any toys he was given to other kids, or to the op-shop. Zephyr had never been interested in toys. Patrick had made him wooden blocks of various sizes when he was little and handed down his childhood Lego, but they were the extent of his toys. When Zeph was given any money he always bought himself rope or a hammer or a torch.

On the road, the idea of toylessness was easy to instil: we simply had no room. When we visited libraries, op-shops or people's homes, Woody played with toys. He especially loved trolleys, wagons, scooters and prams. And he knew, at the end of these visits, that the toys were returned and we left without them. There was never an argument because the parameters were established from the beginning. While some toys may encourage imaginative play, social skills and dexterity, they can also infantilise as they take the child away from the action of the everyday world around them. We didn't want this for our boys.

When we arrived in Red Rock on the mid-north coast, a string of challenging events beset us. As we hurriedly put up tents and inflated sleeping mats at dusk, 20 or so metres from the beach, we were set upon by the local mozzie population. In some regions Aboriginal people burned the leaves of native cherry to keep mozzies at bay, but just as my tin-whistling would have given our game away, so too would lighting a fire. We went to sleep that night with the sound of the waves in the background and the whine of mosquitoes at the fore. The next morning we woke to a flat tyre on the tandem and a heavy dew that permeated our tents and bedding. We were always dry inside our tents, even under heavy rain, but condensation knew no barriers. On such mornings, we sometimes packed up our gear wet and made sure we found camp by mid-afternoon so we could dry our things out, but that morning Woody and I draped nearly everything we all owned on a fence that neighboured our campsite while Patrick patched his tube.

Before we left home we had invested in thorn-proof tubes and tyres for both bikes. But after 2000 kilometres, our back tyres were beginning to wear thin. We didn't know it at the time, but that flat tyre was the first of many we would have to patch on both back wheels as we rode along the Pacific Highway towards Grafton. It was one of our more difficult days on the road, when it seemed nothing could go right. Woody and I had colds, I was fighting off a persistent UTI, we had to navigate numerous stretches of dangerous, bike-unfriendly roads with little or no shoulder, and to top things off, we had a stiff headwind all the way. It took us a whole day to ride a mere 50 kilometres; in good conditions we could ride as much as 15 kilometres an hour.

People often asked us if there were ever moments when we wanted to turn around and come home. My mind always picked that early April day we rode towards Grafton, arriving at 6 pm, starving and exhausted, instead of at lunchtime as we had aimed.

Despite that, my answer was always a defiant no. We were learning, physically and emotionally, that after the difficult struggle up, what fun the downhills were. By facing such setbacks, we were learning resilience, patience and bouncebackability. Even though such days invoked swearing, headaches and sometimes tantrums in us adults, we wouldn't have skipped over them for anything. We didn't seek out hardship, but we were certainly thankful for them, especially when they were over and we were curled up in our tents at the end of the day. Despite how the hours of riding sometimes dragged on, daylight always faded, the night always found us, and sleep always came.

Some days we set up camp at dusk and packed up at first light to ensure we weren't disturbed by dog walkers, rangers or do-gooders who might feel compelled to dob us in. Sometimes we raced against mozzies, sometimes our own fatigue. In Lawrence, 32 kilometres north of Grafton, we brazenly set up camp in the early afternoon beside the Clarence River as we raced the storm clouds that were making their way towards us. We spent three wet and windy but very peaceful days in Lawrence.

While our tents took a mighty battering from two huge storms, we remained mostly dry and warm.

That first afternoon after we set up camp, we tarped over the bikes and walked to the local pub. While we sipped our ales and watched the downpour from the deck, we met local farmer Rex, whose nearby family farm grows sugarcane. Like us, Rex's family avoids processed sugar in their diet, and like us, he sang the praises of cold-extracted honey, which we thought was pretty ironic for a sugar farmer. We'd read that though some form of sugar is naturally found in many foods, by itself it contains no nutrients, proteins, enzymes or healthy fats, just empty and quickly digested calories that actually draw minerals from the body during digestion.

It was refreshing to hear Rex agree with us as to why sugar should be avoided, even though his livelihood depended on it. Despite his protestations 'I'm not a greenie!', Rex shared other environmental concerns with us, such as bottled water. He couldn't work out why environmentalists don't focus more on disposable waste, especially plastic pollution, and why water bubblers were not more widespread in Australia.

Aah, water bubblers. A topic close to our hearts.

In 2007 when Patrick's Just Free Water campaign was in full swing, he spent a day walking the Melbourne CBD streets counting the number of drinking fountains. He drew a map to record them and whether they were in working order, which he then sent to the City of Melbourne. His map revealed that there was only one working fountain for every 40,000 people living, working or visiting in the city. Four years later, Artist as Family walked the same streets auditing bubblers, and again, plotted them on a hand-drawn map. Even though there were more people using the CBD on a daily basis than four years earlier, our audit showed there was now one drinking fountain per 20,205 people, a marked improvement. When bubblers aren't available it encourages people to buy water. Our home-region had become a considerable area for water mining to supply this completely unnecessary product.

In Lawrence, between downpours, we walked the wide quiet streets counting trees with edible fruit on them. Our two most exciting finds were guavas, which we ate soft and picked slightly underripe so they would keep, and publicly planted pecans.

After our hellish day riding to Grafton we were absolutely exhausted. I don't think we realised just how much until we arrived in Lawrence. And I don't think we realised just how much we needed the pecans to rejuvenate us, until Patrick scaled the large tree just near our campsite and started dropping the oblong nuts down to Woody and me, who scrambled with delight to catch them. They were the most buttery pecans we'd ever had. The trees weren't naturalised so we couldn't add them to our free tucker list, but rather planted by some kind, forward-thinking folk some forty or so years earlier.

In Lawrence we fished, only pulling small bream from the Clarence, and for the first time we spotted cattle egrets. These lovely white birds have formed a symbiotic relationship with cattle and other large mammals such as horses, eating insects disturbed by them and also removing from their hides, ticks and flies. Of all the birds we rode past, cattle egrets were the most mercurial, taking flight as Woody called out, 'Cattol egwets!' as he spotted them, which he did from Lawrence all the way to northern Queensland.

From Lawrence we pedalled through the lovely town of Maclean, then on to the small coastal town of Yamba, setting up camp on the beach at Hickey Island. The secluded island was named after Bill Hetherington Hickey who spent most of his life in nearby Iluka, but we suspected it was really named after the love bite, aka hickey, which a gazillion sandflies lovingly bestowed upon us.

Apparently there are thirteen different types of sandflies, also called midges and sandfleas, in Yamba, all of which are small and hungry for the blood of cycle-touring swaggies who had not yet built up resistance to their bites. Mosquitoes were also rampant, but where mozzie bites may flare up and itch for a day or so, sandfly bites are small and for us, itched incessantly for weeks. In other places we had camped, we only had to cover up at dusk and dawn to avoid being attacked, but on Hickey Island, they came after us from the moment we arrived to the moment we threw our things into panniers and rode the hell outta there.

We would have liked to have stayed longer in Yamba. The weekly farmers' market was brimming with local organic fresh and bulk produce, and in early 2013, the town's residents created 'Edible Yamba', transforming existing council and business-owned gardens into edible streetscapes in and around the small CBD, from which we harvested salad greens and herbs to add to our lunch and dinner. Unfortunately, free and good food were no match for the town's insect life, so we decided to catch the ferry over to Iluka and ride 15 kilometres north to Woombah, where we had been kindly invited to stay with Deanne, whose sister Sonya we met briefly in Avoca two months earlier.

We rolled onto the ferry and were greeted by the effervescent ferry mistress Linda, who accommodated a family on extra long bikes with great enthusiasm. By the end of the 45-minute journey Linda had invited us to stay in the granny flat behind her house in Iluka, for which we were extremely grateful, as the tandem, whose rear wheel was giving Patrick more trouble, didn't last the short ride from the jetty to Linda's. We were grateful, too, for a warm shower, which we hadn't had for a week.

Iluka was flat and sandfly-free but, unfortunately, also free from a bike shop. The nearest one was in Lismore, 90 kilometres away, which ordinarily we could have ridden in a day or two. We didn't just feel vulnerable on the roads on our bikes, but also without our bikes, as it dawned on us how dependent on cars we still were, as there was no public transport. Fortunately, Deanne, whom we had not yet met, organised to lend us her car, and was even able to borrow a car seat for Woody from a neighbour.

On the drive to Lismore, we passed a cycle-tourer and were mortified that we were not, for this moment of our trip, part of his community. We were even too embarrassed to toot our horn. In Lismore we discovered that our bike problem was bigger than we thought, and we were going to have to wait several days for a part to arrive. The bike issue was the same as we'd had in Colac Colac.

But we didn't mind; we had nowhere else to be. Linda kindly offered us her flat until the bike was sorted. We were thankful for the break. While in Lismore we stocked up on organic produce from one of the town's bulk foodstores in whose window we saw a poster about the Bentley Blockade, an anti-coal seam gas protest happening 15 kilometres west of Lismore that we hoped to join when the tandem was fixed. We had met some exceptional people on our travels. We also craved the opportunity to repay the collective kindness and trust we were constantly being shown.

In Iluka, in Linda's small flat that opened out on to her garden, we were really able to rest. Patrick and I napped in the middle of the day when Woody did, and we didn't have the stresses of having to find power or water or hidden campsites. We didn't have to ride tens of kilometres each day and we didn't have to harden ourselves to the trucks and the traffic zooming by. We took long exploratory walks through the Bundjalung National Park to Iluka Bluff and along the beach. We visited the community garden that Linda helped develop that supplies fresh produce to the local branch of Meals on Wheels. We caught up with our friend Eddy from Melbourne, who caught the ferry over from Yamba, and Patrick met Rhoda Roberts.

'Are you that family that came into town on bikes yesterday?' she had asked Patrick. He was having a cuppa at a table outside a café, reading the paper with Woody and Zero while I was back at our granny flat tidying up. Just before we arrived, Linda's tenants had vacated, leaving quite a mess behind. We said we'd clean the small dwelling in exchange for board. Patrick shared our story with Rhoda and her man Steve. Later we learned that Rhoda was the first Aboriginal presenter on prime-time television and introduced the term 'Welcome to country' in the 1980s.

Since my fall on the day we left home, I was very aware just how public our lives had become. When Woody cried, we couldn't just bundle him into the car and close the doors. When I was having an off day, I couldn't just hide away inside until it passed. When Patrick and I made love or argued or prepared meals, we were always in the public domain.

It was liberating. I liked it the same way I had enjoyed being part of, and witness to, the vibrant street life when I had travelled through Southeast Asia in my twenties. The idea that life could be lived openly, communally and on the streets instead of behind high fences and within walls, curtains drawn, had been such a revelation to me.

Before we left home I wasn't sure how I would cope being outside all the time.

Would I feel exposed? I would.

Would I feel vulnerable? I would.

My middle-class self felt unguarded, but I knew it was important to keep challenging her. I didn't want her to feel frightened, but I did want her to feel free. And sometimes she needed a strong nudge in the direction of autonomy, which was one of the reasons I knew this trip, however crazy it had sounded initially, was the best thing for her.

Everywhere we went, we were visible. We were that family on bikes, and were constantly approached with questions, comments, concerns and goodwill. I loved it; I loved the social aspect, meeting so many different kinds of people all the time, sharing our story and hearing theirs.

I loved all the different questions: does Zero ever jump out of his basket? (No.) What do you do for school? (What better school is there than life on the road?) How many flat tyres have you had? (Half a dozen.) Where do you sleep at night? (We stealth-camp.) How much water can you carry? (5 litres.) Where are you going? (North.) Are you writing a book? (Yes.)

Sometimes it could take us a few hours to get anywhere. I honestly never minded; I loved people's enthusiasm. But after 2200 kilometres, I was worn out. I needed a break from the mozzies, from the heat of the day, from the rain at night, from the wind, from being seen all the time.

In Iluka we had time to explore, to walk, to read and draw and journal and blog. And time to experiment. Since learning about the invasive and prolific garden escapee asparagus fern from the Tuncurry Dune Care group, we were keen to learn if the small oblong tubers were edible. We were excited by the possibility of breaking the news: hungry family discovers asparagus fern is edible. But we were wary too, having read that when eaten, the berries of the plant cause intestinal discomfort and contact with the sap causes skin irritation. But there was nothing online about the tubers.

After digging up a plant with dozens of the small tubers, Patrick picked one and nibbled at it, with no immediate adverse reaction. Several hours later he cooked up three small tubers in a pan with butter, which he ate half of, noting they produced an almost metallic taste, which concerned him a little, so he didn't eat anymore. Five or so hours later he started experiencing slight indigestion, gas and a tightening of the stomach, bordering on mild cramps, which then developed into more significant cramping, though not severe enough that I was worried about him. But they were acute enough that we could say for certain that asparagus fern tubers are not edible, at least in the form in which we prepared them. We were disappointed – what better way to mitigate the spread of this aggressive plant than to turn it into food – but relieved that a trip to the hospital wasn't necessary as part of our empirical research.

We had other ideas to investigate. When the tandem was repaired, we hitched our panniers onto our bikes and thanked Linda and her son Nicholas for hosting us so graciously. We left Iluka feeling restored, open to, ready for, and craving the possibilities of our next chapter.

Camp Liberty

— Patrick —

BENTLEY
17 April 2014 to 6 May 2014

'What's that? There ... Those lights... See 'em? Radio it in. Where's the radio? Who's on Vigil tonight?'

'I am,' I said, watching the lights of a lone car moving through a forested road about 4 kilometres to our north. It was around two in the morning and a small group of us were huddled around a low fire. A few others sat together several metres away, looking out to the lights. It was an excellent vantage point. A light air frost hung above us. My face and legs were warm and dried by the burning wood, but my back was damp and freezing. I got a little way from the fire to see better. Some joined me. My shift had started at midnight, and various people had come and gone over the past two hours.

'Who are you?'

'Patrick. G'day.'

'Can you see those lights? They're trying to get around the back of the camp. Radio it in.'

'Vigil C to Camp Liberty. Over.'

I waited a few minutes. The woman directing me was short and fiery, spoke in a thick Irish accent and was wrapped in a heavy blanket. She seemed experienced in this sort of thing.

'Vigil C to Camp Liberty, do you copy? Over,' I repeated.

It was approaching late April. With the weather changing and the first really cold days of the year the Lismore op-shops had been raided for blankets, jackets, gloves, scarves and beanies. The first week at the camp had been hot. But it had turned quickly and was now icy at night. I was kicking myself for not taking a blanket when one was offered to me earlier in the day. A static crackling eventually broke in over the sparkling clear night.

'Go ahead, Vigil C.'

'Solo car driving forest road northwest of Gates A and B. Over.'

It had taken me some time to be able to speak so factually into a radio. When I first started doing these shifts a few weeks ago I would have used twenty more words. The infamous Bentley Blockade, where we were now living and working, was the perfect 'shed' for us to put away our bikes and have another break from the road.

'Copy that, Vigil C. We have a Wallaby checking it out. Over.'

Camp Liberty

'Copy that Camp Liberty. Over and out.'

I put the radio back on my lap and continued looking out west along the Bentley–Kyogle Road. I had been instructed to look for anything suspicious, but mostly for a line of headlights coming from the west. All the alarms were in place; the camp would be woken and we'd have a flood of people in position well before the police arrived. But all it took was for a vigil to miss the call, fall asleep or let their radio battery go flat and we'd be in trouble. That's why there was supposed to be two vigils for each shift. One could run a flat battery back to Camp Liberty a kilometre away, and replace it while one could stay on the post and use a fog horn if necessary as back-up. There was also less likelihood of falling asleep with two. Tonight I had seven for company.

'They're looking for a back road into the drill site,' said the same woman. She was pretty stoned, and seemed to have a certain command over the group. I'd never seen her before, not that that was surprising at Bentley. People were streaming in and out all day and night.

The car kept edging its way along the ridge. I didn't think it was such a big deal. I'd had enough nights doing vigil duty to realise that this wasn't all that exceptional. After the car's lights disappeared and the Wallaby had radioed in that it was one of our mob doing a patrol, things settled down and everyone returned to the fire. I declined the communal joint that was passed around, and each time I did it seem to put people a little more on edge.

'You a cop?' the blanketed woman started on me.

'Yes, I am,' I said laughing, prodding the fire with a stick. 'I rode into camp with my family on our bicycles a few weeks ago as part of a strategic undercover operation. Even our toddler is in on it.'

'Aw, you that bike family?' said a guy in his early twenties, and a few people made some mumbles of recognition.

This seemed to be enough to change the conversation. I didn't know any of these folk. I had done shifts and double shifts at each of the three gates before, but usually with just one other. This was the first time I encountered a bunch of stoners taking up residence at a vigil post.

Earlier in the day there had been talk at Camp Liberty, the main campsite where we had temporarily made our home with about 600 others, that the police could possibly show that morning, perhaps at dawn. Large numbers of the state's special taskforce had been bussed to the area for the notorious annual marijuana festival at Nimbin dubbed MardiGrass. Some protestors said it made good sense for the police to try to bust up the blockade while all those human resources were already in the region. There was another desperate plea put out to not bring drugs or alcohol into the camp. Police sniffer dogs had been parading the streets of Nimbin all weekend and they could easily be brought out to Bentley.

'Wouldn't the media love the drama of a drug bust,' Meg said on hearing the news.

We were at the washing-up tent, racking dishes into the steriliser. Woody and Zero were hanging around the fire with other dogs, kids and parents. Woody was the sort of kid you could leave around a fire and not worry about. He'd made friends with a little girl called Cleo, and her mum Talia and us would take it in turns to mind each other's children while we took on a shift.

'It would certainly undo a lot of the work going on here,' I responded.

What little traditional media had covered the blockade so far had failed to capture the diverse spirit of the people at Bentley. Twitter, Instagram, Facebook and the blogosphere, on the other hand, were not only doing this better, they were also building our numbers on a daily basis. People were streaming into the camp, registering their mobile numbers on the Red Alert list and either setting up their tents or returning home to wait for the call. When we arrived, 4000 people were on the list – teachers, farmers, small business operators, students, musicians, retired baby-boomers, dedicated activists and travellers like us. That number swelled to 7000 in the three weeks we were there.

The message was pretty clear: unconventional gas mining was poor science run by a cowboy industry. There was no guarantee that the cocktail of toxic chemicals used in the fracking – hydraulic fracturing – process could be contained when injected at high pressure into the subterranean shale rock to release the gas. Well known pollutants such as lead, uranium, mercury, formaldehyde and radium are used as well as ethylbenzene, toluene and xylenes, which all have harmful effects on the central nervous system. Around the world, water supplies were being polluted and people and animals were falling sick. Governments had thrown caution out the window; it was left to the people to protect their region's groundwater and air quality.

There was consensus among those who were attending the dawn and dusk meetings each day that this was a drug- and alcohol-free blockade, that it wasn't a festival, despite all the touring bands giving free concerts to keep spirits high. But the few who ignored the constant pleas and all the signs posted everywhere weren't attending the meetings.

'Why did that car slow down?' said Blanket Woman. 'They've gone down Naughtons Gap Road … there …' she pointed. 'They've turned off their lights. Torch! Who's got the torch?'

She took off down the embankment with another blanket-clad dude and we could soon see them spotlighting down on the road. It occurred to me then that this 'noidy bunch had spent the last few days at Mardi-Grass and were still on a bender. By 3 am the abattoir workers were changing shifts, so a number of cars were driving in both directions, cutting through the thick air in a melancholic amble from the slaughterhouse to home, or with an unhurried will to get to work.

The stars were wondrous. I'd already witnessed half a dozen of them shooting while keeping vigil on these nights and each time I'd made a secret wish. On this night, when a star flashed from the northeast with its burning tail brightly dying, I made the wish for the stoners to all bugger off to bed.

Blanket Woman and her friend scrambled back up the bank, calling out it was just someone getting dropped off below at Gate C. She was working herself into quite a state, and her cohort were getting fairly worked up too. I sensed they were really courting drama. I was more interested in the lights I could now see emanating from the Rural Fire Service building about three kilometres down the road. I called it in to Camp Liberty.

The RFS local branch had initially turned down the police request to use their building as a communications hub, but we'd heard a few days earlier that decision was overturned by the RFS central powers in Sydney.

'You can't have local people making local decisions, where will that lead to?' Jarrah, who ran the first-aid tent, scoffed.

In a survey conducted by Southern Cross University, 87 per cent of the shire had voted against coal seam and tight sands gas mining. If the company Metgasco got its way, the farming locality of Bentley, just west of Lismore, would have its first tight sands gas mine. TSG is a worse threat to human and environmental health than CSG as it requires fracking all of the time, whereas CSG exploration does not. It is at the exploration phase that fracking takes place. Metgasco had 1000 mine sites earmarked for exploration in the area. The longer we held the gates, the more Metgasco's share price fell. The broad-based community consensus meant that the state's hand was pretty much tied. The political class was caught up defending civil ideals – business law, growth-economics – believing these anthropocentric abstractions justified a case for exploiting and poisoning the land. Counter to this we maintained a very physical protectorship of it. It would take an army to move us.

We were therefore planning for a great show of police numbers, including riot police. The first time they tried to break up the camp several weeks before we arrived, a red alert was sent out and around three thousand people showed up. The few hundred police that came could do little but stand around and talk to the protectors. It was a peaceful stand-off and because of this and how social media presented this first victory, Bentley gained more and more support, even among the local police force, many of whom didn't want to see their land fracked. Some even leaked us useful intelligence, giving me the idea to launch my seditious Australian Police Against Fracking page on Facebook. The local coppers and their families had just as much to lose as anyone else.

But both sides had their informants, and at the meetings the protector running it would give a cheerio to those working undercover in the camp. When we told Zeph what was going on at Bentley – the late-night vigils, the espionage, the campfires and gangs of kids – he longed to be back with us. It would have been another important experience for him.

Local organic farmers delivered boxes of freshly picked vegetables and fruit daily. People from all over the region were dropping off produce from their own gardens and farms, as well as baked foods, firewood, warm clothes and blankets, and anything they'd read on the shoutout texts and social-media pages being sent from Camp Liberty's communications tent. The large kitchen tent in the camp was a miraculous place of organisation, filled with talented cooks who were used to preparing food for hundreds of people. We all ate so well. But it was also one of the places where people were most vulnerable to burning out. As I was.

These double night shifts were a bit taxing on someone who had become used to going to bed at sunset and rising at dawn. But they would have been fine if only I could have slept solidly during the day. When I got back to our little camp, after meeting Meg, Zero, Woody and any number of our new friends for breakfast, I would clamber into bed and listen to the many sounds of camp life, my mind refusing to shut down and rest. I would nod off and then a car or van would pull up and people would start shouting to one another above the engine.

Meg had specifically chosen our site because it was away from the main noise of the camp, so she could put Woody down for his day sleep without being disturbed. But the longer we were at Camp Liberty the more the land, which had been indefinitely loaned to us by the altruistic farmer who neighbours the mine site, filled up with protectors.

A month before we arrived at Bentley, the upper house of the Victorian parliament amended the *Summary Offences Act* to effectively make it an anti-protest law, an amendment aimed at long-term blockading. Other states followed suit, introducing similar measures. Part of the reason for calling ourselves protectors was to shift the language while the legal goalposts were being moved. But protector was a more apt title anyway. That is why the farm's three gates were permanently blocked, to keep mining equipment from entering. The property owner who sold out to the gas company, and who was set to make a considerable amount of money if gas was found on his land, still had access to his paddocks. Every time he or his family members turned up, Gate B was unlocked and we made way.

'Camp Liberty to Vigil B. Please be respectful to Mr Graham as he passes. Over.'

I tossed and turned. Slept for a little while, and was woken again. I lay there thinking about the diversity of people and politics at Bentley. For many, fracking was the tipping point. People who'd never stood defiant before the police now knew they couldn't avoid it. Capitalism had finally become so utterly reckless that it was willing to poison people's water, soil and air for short-term gain. Around the fires at Camp Liberty, near the kitchen and elders' tents, we'd commune at meal times. The presence of Bundjalung and other first-nation peoples in the camp spoke of the long lineage of stewardship and care on this particular country. We were all part of that succession now. Githabul tribe elder Kevin 'Yillah' Boota and his family were among the most prominent of those who held a significant connection to the land. We listened to Uncle Kevin's rousing words around the campfire.

'The government has always failed Aboriginal people, now it was also failing you white mob. This is a chance to work together, on common goals, on common ground. To put away our petty differences and work together.'

I was developing a man-crush on Uncle Kevin; his eldership in the camp doubled my resolve and commitment. I took on double shifts not just in response to Kevin but as payment for my family's food. Bentley was a non-monetary economy in action. Only those doing shifts were allowed to eat for free, otherwise donations were expected. I loved that Bentley was run on a gift economy. I'd often wondered how such an economy could work on a larger scale than what we'd established in our community gardens back home. Now we were living within such a model.

Because Woody was still so dependent on Meg it was difficult for her to take on many shifts on her own. I needed to work for both us adults to feel like we were fairly contributing. We shared some of the shifts, tag-parenting between feeds at the first-aid tent, the washing-up tent and the info tent. Meg and Woody spent time at the children's tent, which was the camp's creche. Meg was one of the parents to establish a set of procedures so that once the alarm was raised, the children were protected and kept from harm's way should the police turn up. Unless they had a warrant the police couldn't come into Camp Liberty, and it was widely discussed and agreed upon that no children would be allowed at any of the gates once the alarms were raised. Meg and a handful of other parents who had Working with Children cards would become the carers while other parents were up at the gates singing songs, making human walls or locking on to mining or police vehicles or one of the many deeply buried concrete objects.

We loved the self-organising nature of Bentley. No one person was in charge. Most decisions were made by a collective commonsense. While there was disagreement, we were seeing participatory democracy at work.

One night I turned up to vigil at C and found there were already two guys on duty. However Gate C, down on the road, was short a Simmo for the night. Simmo was code for anyone who locked themselves on to some impossibly difficult-to-remove assemblage. Before I thought about what the role meant I agreed to do it and was duly instructed into the art. If Simmos weren't ready at a gate it meant that the police could quickly overwhelm, clear and occupy one of the three entrance ways. Then the drilling rig could be brought in.

Simmos were important to hold the gate until the hordes arrived. A Buddy was assigned to each Simmo. Their role was to bring them food, water and anything else they needed. If a Simmo was to be locked on for hours their Buddy may even need to change their nappy. There was a lot of experience in the camp and every scenario was being considered and managed, but sometimes positions were short or people failed to show up. That night I was a Simmo-in-training, without a Buddy, let alone a nappy.

I can't remember the name of the tall skinny guy who showed me the ropes, but I immediately liked him. He was intelligent, funny and serious. He produced a spare set of chain lengths and lock, and demonstrated how to attach it to my wrist. While my fellow Simmos slept next to their lock-on points, he showed me where mine was. He proceeded to rake back old grass, lift a rock and scratch back the dirt to reveal a plate of cardboard covering the top of a buried pipe. It sank down into the ground an arm's length and was concreted in at the base. Where the bottom of the pipe met the concrete footing a thick steel eyelet protruded, where I was to hook my lock.

'You need to be able to finger your lock around the bar while your arm is down the hole. But whatever you do don't lock it unless the police arrive. Even then, you might just want to wait and only fully lock on if it looks like they've arrived to break up the party.'

It was good advice. It would take hours to get someone out of one of these lock-on points — that was the idea.

'You may want to practise getting your arm down the hole and the lock into position. It takes time to perfect the movements, you don't want to panic.'

He also gave me advice about my ID. 'If the cops arrive at dawn, they could surprise you so quickly you don't have time to organise what you have in your wallet or whether you want anything on you at all. Police will go through all your various IDs and could possibly use the information to build data on you. They could also use the contents – receipts, family photos, club memberships – to work you in a police interview. Apart from your name and address, you don't need to say a single thing more. But they'll work you.'

He sounded like the voice of experience.

He left me to my homework, and I thought about the best possible thing to do. I'd heard from other activists that by cooperating with the police they're more likely to let you go earlier. But then, I thought, if I only had to give them my name and address, I could do that verbally. I hid my wallet a little way from the gate and returned to my point to settle in for the night.

Despite having a home, my name wasn't actually on the title. As others were living in my house and I wasn't on any title or rental agreement anywhere in the world, I actually didn't reside at any address. Jesus! I hadn't realised it before. I actually live at no fixed address *and* I don't drive a car. No need for photo ID. I ran through the scenario at the police station a hundred times, perfecting my statement.

'My name is Patrick Jones. I live at no fixed address and I don't own a car.'

Oh my god. I'm free! The idea enveloped me. I was lying on cold ground with a blanket to keep the frost off my clothes, my right wrist wrapped in chains resting on top of my lock-on point, which at any moment I could chain myself to, and I'd never felt more liberated.

Camp Liberty

'Patrick Jones. No fixed address. No car.'

It was no haiku, but it was probably the best poem I'd ever written. Getting the intonation right as I would say it was going to be really important.

God, what a middle-class wanker I am. I eventually fell asleep wondering if the vigils were awake up there, a hundred metres above the gate, doing their job, or whether we'd all be woken to the scream of police megaphones, stomping boots and general chaos with no warning. I'd remember where my wallet was, but how was I going to tell Meg how to find it if I was arrested and couldn't return to Bentley?

Did I even need a wallet?

I awoke to be relieved by another Simmo and wandered back to meet Meg, Zero and Woody at Camp Liberty and to tell them of my night. I felt initiated into the clan of Simmos, and was excited to put my hand up for more of this work. It certainly got my adrenalin going. But after talking it through with Meg, I decided that I was of more use to my family not arrested and separated from them in a police cell. Although Meg left the decision to me, I felt better if I continued my work as a vigil. I was no longer twentysomething with only myself to think about.

'Camp Liberty to Vigil C. Over.'

'Vigil C. Go ahead Camp Liberty,' I enunciated back into the radio. I wanted to be the best bloody vigil ever to exist.

'Vigil C. Just wanting an update on the RFS building. Over.'

'Lights now out at RFS. Over.'

'Copy that. Over and out.'

In the half-hour or so the lights remained on in the RFS building the stoned speculation of what might be going on in there was unbelievably tiresome. It could have been anyone – the captain of the service having an affair or he couldn't sleep and had thought of something to do in the middle of the night. Maybe it was the cleaner. It was better in moments like this, I was told by more experienced campaigners, to keep cool on the radio, just report facts and not get carried away with speculation.

'They're setting up communications. It's close now. Any day. Maybe this morning,' ranted Blanket Woman.

Dawn was approaching and I tried to focus on the road and not the fireside talk. The very stoned 22-year-old business management student I was supposed to be doing the vigil with was trying to engage me in his theory of how to fix the world. From where I was sitting he hadn't really got all that far in his thinking, and I felt trapped by the most wise, the most brilliant, the most original thinker of all time who was foaming the most unbelievable diarrhoea from his mouth.

'Have you asked an elder about your theory?' I asked provocatively. 'Have you run it by Uncle Kevin?' I asked more seriously. 'Perhaps he would have something to say about your exploiting other planets and moons and their resources, and the hyper-tech world of the future you're envisaging.'

'Not "exploiting",' he said, a little hurt. 'We're entering a new era of consciousness. We're about to learn what real energy is. The technology is coming.'

I'd heard the technology-will-save-us myth a thousand times, in all its variations, although this New Age angle was not as familiar. In ten years' time, I thought gloomily, he'll be an executive in a boardroom making decisions about someone else's resources, somewhere. And he'll draw on what he learnt at Bentley. My patience had worn thin. The saddest diatribes were circling around me.

'It won't matter what colour you are,' he proceeded, 'it's about a higher state that …'

'Oh, would you just stop talking shit!' I yelled at him, and got up and left the fire.

This gave everyone the chance to discuss my problems, which collectively boiled down to the fact I wasn't smoking dope. For a while things were a little awkward, but my outburst had the desired effect. People began to drift off to their tents or fall asleep by the fire, and I returned to warm up and continue my vigil.

Before Bentley, I'd never had a problem with *Cannabis indica*, and would occasionally enjoy a joint with a friend. We would even include it in our research (as a medicinal plant) if we came across it naturalised in our travels, only with a warning note: Dickhead-inducing if mistreated.

'Camp Liberty to Vigil C. Radio check. Over.'

'Vigil C to Camp Liberty. Loud and clear. Over and out.'

The dawn came with no show from police. My replacements came and dreamily I walked the 700 metres up to Gate A to catch the tail end of the morning's meeting and the singing. On the previous morning, just before dawn broke, I had watched Uncle Kevin holding proceedings. We were still and quiet around his sacred fire, listening to the song of the kookaburras. It was so simple, so straightforward. The day begins in Bundjalung country with these lyrical voices. No one speaks over this moment. No one dominates. We were part of the day, listening to the other communities of the living that inhabit the land.

'How can you quantify the clarity of this thinking?' I said to Meg over breakfast. 'How can something as robotic as NAPLAN (the National Assessment Program for Literacy and Numeracy) and the way we school our kids indoors for long periods teach them about such regard? How can you argue against a mindset whose power comes from a place where birdsong has been trafficked over and just one species of animal dominates as though this is perfectly normal?'

Meg ran her fingers through my hair. 'Go to bed my darling, you're exhausted.'

I walked down through the brightly flapping flags and banner-lined laneways of Camp Liberty, careful not to stub my toes on any number of the basalt floaters that had pushed their way up through the red soil like little hard boils, and found our tents. Meg had hung out our bedding to dry in the morning's sun as the night's condensation had been sponged up by them. I placed my

Camp Liberty

little mattress down on the damp sour autumn grasses, got into my sleeping bag and tried to sleep. I turned over and stared out across the long paddock of cows that ran down to the tree-lined creek, stoned on fatigue.

Becoming north

— Meg —

BENTLEY to TOWNSVILLE
2000 KILOMETRES
6 May 2014 to 14 August 2014

'No way!' Patrick screamed, looking at the phone. 'Amazing!'

'What is it?!'

We'd had a break from our bikes, but after three weeks we nonetheless left Bentley exhausted. I had enjoyed our time there and had loved the vitality of camp life but was desperate for some down time. I have never been a good sleeper and have trained myself to get by on little sleep. But all those nights Patrick stayed up on vigil took their toll on me, too. Each evening he walked up to the gates I felt as though he was going off to battle. I would only feel myself truly relax when I saw him for breakfast the next day.

We were riding back to the blockade with renewed

energy from Mullumbimby, where we had had spent a week recuperating with our friends Vanessa, Chris and Willem. The intelligence from Camp Liberty was that several hundred riot police were due to arrive in two days' time and we wanted to be there for the showdown. Ten kilometres out of Mullumbimby, we pulled off the road. A week earlier, going in the opposite direction, we had picked up Dee, our first hitchhiker, on the back of the tandem. She was apprehensive but as we'd been looking out for a hitchhiker to fill Zeph's seat since his departure, we wouldn't take no for an answer. She reluctantly put on Zeph's helmet, saying she hadn't been on a bike in years, but by the time we pulled up outside the café where she worked, she thanked us heartily and farewelled us like old friends. This time we stopped as we had the choice of several roads to take back to the blockade. We turned on our phone to check a map and before long it was dinging with messages from family and friends asking us to confirm whether the news was indeed true.

Patrick read out a Gasfield Free Northern Rivers alert: '"Metgasco's licence has been suspended, the police operation cancelled and the matter has been referred to the Independent Commission Against Corruption." I can't believe it!'

'Oh my god! Oh my god! Oh my god!'

Woody may not have understood what was behind his parents' joyous yells and whoops, but I'm sure he picked up that it was something pretty significant.

'We won! We bloody well won!'

Becoming north

All over Mullumbimby, people had been doing what they could to support the blockade. The food co-op where Vanessa worked was accepting donations of food and money and were themselves gifting large amounts of produce, and community noticeboards were listing carpools for people offering or wanting lifts out to Bentley, 70 kilometres away. There was a Mothers' Day breakfast fundraiser that Vanessa helped organise, which we went along to, and when we had the tandem serviced, the bike-shop owner waived the charge when Patrick told him we had been at the blockade and were about to ride back.

After calling friends and family to confirm the news, we rode on to Brunswick Heads, several kilometres away. As our bikes were covered in anti-fracking slogans, cars were tooting us as we came into town, cafés were booming celebratory music and had messages of congratulations on their sandwich boards out the front. It was such a thrill to be part of the festivities in Brunswick Heads, because after much deliberating we decided not to return to Bentley. It would've been a 140-kilometre round trip and the nights were starting to get really cold; we were reluctant to travel south again. We'd packed up our tents before we left Camp Liberty so apart from joining in the celebrations, we didn't need to return.

My initial dread of camping every night seemed absurd to me now. I had enjoyed the luxury of a bed at Chris and Vanessa's, a kitchen and a bath too, but after a week I was ready to farewell our dear friends and the privilege of hot water and return to the uncertainty of the road and living outdoors.

I missed the breeze on my face at night in the tent, I missed the clarity of the birdsong in the morning, I missed cooking on coals, I missed living unselfconsciously without a mirror, and I missed watching Woody explore his surrounds, digging holes, collecting leaves of various shapes and textures, identifying animal scats. I wanted to keep travelling on our bikes forever.

'Do you think you could?' I asked Patrick, as we packed our clothes into our panniers in Vanessa and Chris's spare room.

'Could what?'

'Do you think you could live like this forever?'

'I reckon I could.'

'Me too,' I said looking over at him, smiling.

'Let's ask Yael and Matt if they want to stay longer,' he suggested, talking about the tenants who were renting our house, who by now had become long-distance friends.

After discussing it with Mel and Zeph, we then asked Yael and Matt if they would like to extend their stay by another six months. They had told us how happy they were in Daylesford and we thought this might suit them too.

Six months! I felt giddy with the possibilities this extra time represented. Where would we go? What would we do?

It was in Mullum that we started sending out our 'Letter to elders', which we wrote at Bentley. Several times already we had dropped into Aboriginal cooperatives or cultural centres to ask permission to travel through and camp on their country. One cooperative was closed for a funeral, another time the sole elder was travelling interstate, and once we were asked to put something in writing which would be discussed at the upcoming monthly meeting. Sending a letter ahead seemed like a good plan.

Back home a number of years ago, Jaara elder Uncle Brien Nelson told us about his people's traditional form of barter, the tanderrum, which translates to 'freedom of the bush'. A tanderrum agreement is made when landholders give travellers temporary access to their country and resources in exchange for gifts, which was what we were seeking.

We were looking forward to exploring the sunny state of Queensland, its rainforests and beaches, but we were also apprehensive, especially about its politics and the police. We had been warned that when we crossed the border people wouldn't be as friendly towards dogs off leads, and we'd heard a story of a cycle-tourist who had been stopped by a highway patrol who tipped out the contents of his panniers and emptied his water bottles on the side of the road, supposedly looking for contraband. We had seen a Queensland map of all the coal-seam gas mine sites and were frightened of breathing toxic air and having no option but to drink polluted water. And we'd heard that Queensland drivers don't care that much about bikes, despite their new state law maintaining that in a 60 km/h or less zone motorists must leave a minimum of one metre when passing a cyclist, and 1.5 metres where the speed limit is over 60 km/h.

It was only 50 kilometres from Brunswick Heads to the Queensland border but to us it seemed a world away. We were intrigued as to what adventures Queensland would hold for us, but we were also in no hurry to leave the beautiful lands of the northern rivers of New South Wales.

When we decided not to return to Bentley, we called fellow protector Eka, who had previously invited us to stay. We arranged to visit her in South Golden Beach, about 12 kilometres north of Brunswick Heads. Our friend Brett from Kempsey was going to join us at Bentley, but came to Eka's instead. He would soon be heading to Liberia in West Africa to manage the Médecins Sans Frontières Ebola hospital.

We travelled with Brett for a fortnight through the lushest country, stopping to pick naturalised banana passionfruit, more roadside guavas and to buy eggs, herbs, fruit or preserves at farmgate stalls that were sometimes just an esky and a hand-written sign.

In Uki, we set up camp on the banks of the Tweed River and were soon visited by friendly local Tim, who with his partner Ahliya joined us for a dinner of sweet potatoes wrapped in river-soaked Bangalow palm leaves cooked on coals. While dodging smoke from our little fire, our musical guests serenaded us with their homespun tunes, Tim playing his guitar.

'We're trying to smash the record,' Patrick joked with our friends Belinda and Cecile as we arrived at their house in Murwillumbah, just 13 kilometres on from Uki, 'of travelling Australia at the slowest possible speed.'

The unhurried pace agreed with us. We took our time to pick roadside mandarins, making videos of each other as we flew down the hills, stopping to fill our water bottles in the sparkling creeks. Brett rode with us for a few more days, staying with a mutual friend at the Gold Coast. The second most populated city in Queensland, its theme parks, high-rise buildings, chain restaurants, nightclubs and merchandise stores may have provided relief for other travelling families, but despite the beautiful long sandy beaches we couldn't leave quickly enough. We took a quiet service road that ran beside the motorway to Brisbane, because bikes were not permitted – the first and last time we came across such a prohibition.

In the West End of the state's capital we camped for several nights in a house with a productive urban permaculture garden belonging to another Tim, whom we had met via Warm Showers. Some Warm Showers hosts required a few weeks' notice, some more, but Tim only needed a day or two. He took us to the Northey Street City Farm, its market garden and food forest, where we tasted soursop, a fruit indigenous to Central America and a relative of pawpaw. The day before we left, we ran a rooster-killing workshop in Tim's backyard with his friends. That night we cooked the bird with some City Farm veggies and feasted with everyone around the kitchen table. In this particular share-house the permaculture revolution was well underway.

It was afternoon by the time we braved our way east across the busy streets of Brisbane to catch a barge across to Minjerribah, North Stradbroke Island. We were joined by Ko, Brisbane Tim's friend, who brought his bike along too. We thought we'd find a park and bunker down for the night, but instead Ko called his work colleague, Shelley, who generously invited us to stay in her family's Dunwich home. In the morning, while we harvested macadamias from her tree, we talked about mining. Not CSG this time but sand, as Minjerribah is the second largest sand island in the world, after Fraser Island. Shelley told us that the local sand-mining industry was being challenged by people in the community who wanted to move towards more sustainable enterprises.

We spent a week on the island swimming and fishing, going to the Point Lookout talent night at the bowls club, joining a yoga class, and hiding out in the bush. We camped again with our favourite bearded cycle-tourer Tom and Uki Tim, watched humpback whales migrating north, and collected numerous foods to add to our growing list, including chickweed, clover, pigface flowers, more guavas, midyim berries, black nightshade, flax lily berries, warrigal greens, purslane, pilchards that had washed up on the beach, fish Patrick speared or line-caught that we cooked over coals for lunch and dinner (grey morwong, sand whiting, swallowtail dart), and bags of eugaries (pipis) which we dug up with our foraging tool at low tide and cooked on coals. These were such a treat and a traditional food of the Quandamooka people.

After a few run-ins with island rangers, who politely asked our merry cycling tribe to move on from our unofficial campsites, it was time to catch the ferry back to the mainland and continue north.

In cities where foraging was more difficult we were forced to buy much of our food. This made us feel like we were taking a backward step from how we lived at home, where we hadn't shopped in a supermarket for years. But finding our own nourishment from the sea and land, and to be able to continue to teach Woody to feed himself, was rewarding and filled us not just with calorific energy, but the enthusiasm to carry on with what we were doing, and to keep spreading the message and sharing our findings with others on our blog.

'Where the hell are we?' Patrick yelled to a herd of cows, as we bumped our way past them on a pitted gravel road, north of Woodford.

'Yeah, cows,' I mocked.

'Yeah cowsh,' Woody echoed.

'Remind me why you put the GPS on bike route?' Patrick asked me, slowing down until we were side by side.

Even though we vowed never to again select 'bike route' on our GPS after we kept getting sent up roads that turned out to be dead-ends, I had clicked it this time instead of 'car route' to see if there was a shorter back road to Maleny. The paper maps that we picked up free from local tourist info centres weren't often detailed enough for the minor roads we sought. Occasionally, but very occasionally, the GPS 'bike route' on my phone was the better option.

'How was I to know it would be mostly gravel and hills this way?' I replied.

'But how can we make the same fucking mistake again?' Patrick snapped.

Not only were we lost, we had to contend with crossing a fast-flowing but passable stream for the first time, an unrelenting sun, and hills so steep I was unable to ride up them even with my pedal-assisted motor on full blast. Luckily we got directions from a dude on a dirt bike because there were no road signs anywhere and the phone was no longer in range. For the first time, I lifted Woody from his seat and asked him to walk up a hill to lighten my load. He kept slipping over on the uneven ground, laughing like a slapstick star in his own movie. Patrick and I were laughing too.

'I'm glad you got us lost, Meg,' Patrick smiled, 'it's so quiet out here.'

After an afternoon's struggle we'd climbed so high that just before Maleny we were offered a remarkable view across to the striking Glass House Mountains that looked like a family of pyramids. We arrived at dusk, completely worn out, and set up camp on a flat piece of grass beside the Obi Obi Creek behind one of the local pubs. We treated ourselves to a counter meal. We must have looked and smelled a fright, but no-one seemed to care. We used the bathroom hand basins to clean ourselves up.

The next morning we wandered into town and came across the Maple Street Co-op, which has been running since 1979, and bought bulk foods to restock our panniers. Oats, pasta, honey, tahini, dried fruit, nuts, seeds and a little fresh produce. People often asked us how much food we carried and we usually answered enough for a day-and-a-half. While it would have been sensible to stick to that, at community-run food co-ops, especially ones where we could buy things in bulk and store them in our own bags and jars, we stocked up so we had enough for several days.

By the time we reached Maleny, all the fears we'd had or negative press we'd heard about Queensland seemed silly to us.

At the community garden behind the co-op we weeded and walked and watered our way around the labyrinthine path, finding, among other things, gotu kola, which according to the co-op newsletter, may be used in the treatment of 'fatigue, anxiety, depression, poor memory, senility, epilepsy, bacterial viral or parasitic infections, trauma and tissue repair, leprosy, circulation problems, tuberculosis, arthritis, rheumatism and skin conditions such as psoriasis'. We munched on this powerful herb that had naturalised in Queensland.

Just as we were leaving the garden we got talking to Garry, a fellow cyclist and gardener who invited us back to his home where he lived with his partner Susan on their large permaculture property. We had a couple of slow and dreamy days there and left with our food panniers bulging even more, with fresh eggs, citrus and other goodies that soon included a haul of slippery jack mushrooms we found on the way out of town. Luckily for us, the road to Kenilworth, our next destination, was nearly all downhill as we descended from 488 metres above sea level to 97.

Woo hoo!

Not long after we left Kenilworth the tandem had more issues. The right gear cable snapped. We pulled over at a public reserve to see whether it was suitable for an emergency camp when David, who lived across the road, appeared and invited us to spend the night. David and Patrick got to work, making the bike rideable by tying off the remaining cable.

The following morning we faced a 60-kilometre ride to the nearest bike shop in Gympie. With just two working gears and a heavier bike than usual, Patrick struggled, especially on one particular stretch that had us climbing to 249 metres above sea level. When he finally reached the summit I was long gone, with our only working phone.

'Why didn't you stop and wait?' Patrick asked, once we were reunited on the side of the road, an hour or so later.

'Woody fell asleep. If I stop, he wakes up.'

'I had no idea where you were! How did you know I was OK? We're a team you know, Meg.'

'I know!' I yelled. 'I was riding as slowly as I could. I wasn't worried about *you*. You're a grown man. Woody's my baby!'

'What if something else happened to the tandem?'

'I knew you'd catch up. And if you didn't, I would have turned around and gone back to look for you.'

'These missing gears have just about killed me. I'd have liked some support.'

We rolled into the large regional town of Gympie for a late lunch. Miraculously we found a bike shop that stocked a tandem-length gear cable. After it was installed, and spending a night in a cheap pub where we smuggled Zero up the back stairs, we were on the road again headed west towards Widgee, 30 kilometres away. Just before the little town we stopped at a mid-week garage sale. The owners were moving to a wetter region because they couldn't afford to keep buying in water.

'Guess what?' I asked Patrick, looking at my phone.

'What?' he said, strapping a little wooden bow and arrow we'd just bought for Woody to the tandem.

'We just got an email from Yael and Matt.'

'And?'

'And they would love to stay longer in our house.'

'Really?' he asked, lifting Woody onto his seat. 'Fantastic!'

'Oh wait.'

'What?'

'They can't do six months, but they can do an extra two and stay till January.'

'Great!' he said, strapping on Woody's helmet, being extra careful not to catch any skin in the clasp, as he had done before.

'It is great, but I'm still disappointed.'

'It means we'll have a few weeks to settle Zeph back home if he's going to start high school next year,' he said, lifting Zero into his basket. At that point it wasn't clear whether Zeph would continue being home-educated or would go to school.

'I know, it's great. But I'm still disappointed it's not for longer.'

'Listen to you now!' Patrick laughed.

'I know! Now I never want to go home.'

Just after we arrived in Hervey Bay, 300 kilometres north of Brisbane, a couple on their bikes approached us, offering us a bag of mandarins from their garden. Kelly and Wendy were full of local knowledge and told us about an abandoned caravan park, which had both a toilet and free barbecue. Only a few weeks earlier a 4-metre long crocodile was sighted on the beach nearby, Kelly told us, marking our entry into the next significant creature zone.

As nearby Fraser Island shelters Hervey Bay from the ocean surf, the water in Hervey Bay is free from waves, ideal for quiet afternoons of fishing. Catching, killing, gutting, eating and admiring fish soon consumed a considerable part of our days. On Urangan Pier, which stretched almost a kilometre out to sea, an elderly Aboriginal lady showed us how to jag baitfish. Each day we set about catching Australian herring and Southern gar, which we happily ate but also used as bait to pull in larger fish.

'What do you think?' I asked Patrick on our last night in Hervey Bay as we lay in our tent just after I'd put Woody to sleep. We had relocated our tents from a week's solitude in the jungle-like old caravan park to the manicured lawns of a nearby youth hostel so we could shower, recharge our devices and do some laundry.

'I say north.'

'Me too,' I squealed, jumping on top to pash him.

We had been travelling for seven months, exactly half of our allotted time away. Leaving Hervey Bay, we had to decide whether we would slowly pedal our way southwards towards home, or continue north, even if it meant catching a train or bus or hitching a ride with a truckie part of the way to get home by January.

Several days later we made camp at the oval in Rosedale. While Patrick and Woody put up tents and I blew up sleeping mats, Zero got to work flushing out and killing three small kitten rabbits from under a shipping container. Many omnivores would have pooh-poohed these undersized animals, but we were thrilled to add them to our meal. Patrick skinned and salted the pelts and put them in the sun to dry, then poached the meat briefly in the billy before removing the bones and tossing the tender flesh through a pasta dish of raw chopped garlic, kale, zucchini, olive oil and salt. It was one of the most delicious dishes we had eaten on our trip.

A few days later the three pelts that Patrick had on the back of his bike were dry.

It was a shame the pelts were too small to keep even Zero warm had we stitched them together as it was freezing in Calliope River. On our first morning, our tents were crunchy with ice. When we were finally bold enough to leave our down sleeping bags, we got to work collecting firewood and making porridge. Later that day we heard that it had been the coldest July night in Queensland for a century. I had been looking at the map of Australia my entire life, and somehow I thought that as soon as we crossed the border from NSW to Queensland, it would instantly be warmer. Perhaps it was all those tourism ads; I hadn't realised just how big Queensland was.

By the time we arrived in the inland city of Rockhampton, we had been on the road for eight months. I was really tired of being so cold every morning. Our bikes needed a thorough service, and apparently so did we.

'Don't talk to them, they're dirty!' a woman hissed to her husband the afternoon we arrived.

We were outside a shopping centre with our bikes and Patrick had just returned with some oats, pasta and bread from the supermarket. Undeterred, the man finished his conversation with us, then went to find his wife.

'We really are the great unwashed,' Patrick laughed.

After some googling we found a solar-powered, dog-friendly motel and booked in for the night. There was a kettle! And a toaster! The windows of our room could be blackened out with thick curtains and the next day we all slept in until 9 am. Our one night there turned into seven, after they offered us a discounted weekly rate we couldn't, and didn't want to, refuse.

We occasionally had people honking their horns or giving us the thumbs up as we rode, just as we sometimes had abuse yelled out as well. Riding on the Bruce Highway north of Rockhampton, it seemed every second car tooted at us or waved encouragingly. We had vehicles slowing down so the kids in the back could yell out hello.

'What's going on?' I asked Patrick when we pulled over to have a break.

'It's so weird,' he replied, laughing.

'I don't know if I'm feeling strong on the bike after a week's rest,' I said, 'or if I'm just feeling spurred on by all the encouragement.'

A few days later we learned the real reason for the tooting and cheering that continued for at least another week. In Rockhampton we had been interviewed on the local ABC radio station and the interview had then been played on ABC *Statewide*, giving it a much broader audience. The recognition boosted our morale, but we were still keen to get the hell off the Bruce. It was so noisy with trucks that Woody and I couldn't hear each other talking or singing.

Leaving Rockhampton, we set our GPS to 'bike route' again, and hoped for the best. An alternative presented itself, which meant we could avoid the Bruce, which Patrick affectionately called Rod – Road of Death.

Finally, it seemed we could relax a little. Woody and I could hear each other as we sang our sugarcane song, riding beside the canefields: 'Sugarcane it's all the same, sugarcane it's all the same, sugarcane it's all the same, Queensland monoculture ...'

When we headed out towards Ridgelands, west of Rockhampton, we had no idea what we were getting ourselves into. We had ridden on gravel roads before, but those times had been shortlived. On the Ridgelands–Glenroy Station Road, there was no pause from the gravel, no shade to ride or rest in, no breeze to cool us down, no passing car even to stir the thickness of the air, no truck stops, no petrol stations, no roadhouses, no houses. And no water.

'I don't think I've ever been this scared,' I said to Patrick on our second day along the road.

I had just slipped on gravel for the third time in about an hour. As with my fall on the day we left home, the panniers provided padding so Woody didn't touch the ground. He was fine, but I wasn't.

'It's OK, gorgeous,' Patrick assured me. 'We're going to be OK.'

He lifted my bike and leant it against a gumtree. Then he took Woody from his seat while I sat on the side of the road sobbing.

'Are you hurt?'

'No. I'm just very, very thirsty,' I said, putting Woody to my breast.

'Have a drink.'

'I just did. But my mouth is still so dry.'

'Have another one. It's OK. We have enough.'

'No, we don't!' I cried.

'We do. We have about 600 ml left.'

'To last us the 40 kilometres to Marlborough? We're not going to make it!'

'Just have another drink, Meg!' he demanded.

So I took a sip. And then I started crying again.

'What is it?'

'I'm crying because I'm crying and I'm losing liquid through my eyes and I can't stop.'

We both laughed, which then turned into more sobbing on my part.

'Meg, we're going to be fine.'

We would have been fine on bitumen, but the unsealed road meant we were going less than half our usual speed. And my falling off the bike was also slowing us down as it meant Patrick had to keep riding back to help me.

'I'm crying, I'm breastfeeding, I'm sweating and I've got my period. I'm losing liquid from every bloody orifice!' I bawled, putting Woody back on the bike.

I had a mouth full of chewed up almonds that I had no saliva to wash down. I spat them out. I was a mess. I wanted to stop right there. To make camp and lie down and not get up for days.

All that rest we'd had in Rockhampton felt completely undone. I wanted a dark room to nap in. I wanted tea! I wanted toast! I even wanted the Bruce Highway.

I had no choice but to keep going. We rode and rode and rode. After a while Woody stopped asking for songs and we both stopped pointing when we saw emus, cows and horses. He fell asleep.

'A farmhouse!' Patrick called out, about an hour later.

'A farmhouse!' I bellowed back, not caring about waking my slumbering cargo (or bikego as we like to say). I parked my bike by the gate and raced up the stairs. I banged on the door and called out, even though it was dark inside and I sensed no one was home. I didn't think they would mind if we helped ourselves to the tap in their yard. We drank and drank and drank, and soon enough we felt restored and positive again, and very, very lucky.

A few days later, after a gentle rest day exploring the mangroves and rockpools at Clairview, where we ate mud whelks and mangrove snails for the first time, we were not so lucky. While having a passionate discussion about the latest Israeli attack on Palestine, Patrick and I rode into each other, trying to hear one another over the roar of trucks on the Bruce.

Woody and I went down. I had fallen off my bike about a dozen times since we'd left home but those times were really just slips. My right hand and knee were bleeding and because of the way we fell, Woody scraped his arm on the road and it was bleeding too.

We were both crying. Patrick righted my bike and I walked it over to some nearby grass. I sat and fed Woody while Patrick fed us rescue remedy and covered us with arnica, green oil antiseptic cream and band-aids.

'You realise this is private property, don't you!' a woman said as she walked towards us. 'That dog over there is a vicious guard dog.' She pointed over her shoulder to a house.

'Is your dog going to come over here?' Patrick asked in disbelief.

It seemed to us we were on a roadside verge. One minute we'd been debating a bloody battle in which innocent people were being killed, schools and hospitals bombed, and the next we were being asked not to sit on somebody's nature strip.

We hobbled into Koumala that afternoon, 67 kilometres on from Clairview, and set up camp behind a toilet block at the sports oval and were in bed before dark. We often caught up with our online correspondence at night: emails, Facebook and Instagram. That night in the tent, I was so sore and tired, I couldn't even hold the phone above my head. It was harvest time and all night long we were woken by sugarcane trains. I was relieved when dawn finally came.

Between Airlie Beach and Townsville we added cocky apple, bush passionfruit, beach cherry, Burdekin plum and Chinee apple to our list, bringing it to nearly 200 species. The first 100 had taken us several years to collate; being on the road, we'd doubled that number in just several months. On our way north towards Townsville we learnt that mangoes, bananas and coconuts had all naturalised to the extent that they were considered weeds.

The pattern of gruelling days, living rough, scavenging for food and being open to chance were punctuated by moments of civil reprieve when we came into the cities. In Townsville, we dusted ourselves off, washed our clothes, compiled photos for our blog and hung out in cafés and the public library, catching up with news from home. Looking like something a feral cat dragged in, we'd approach a city with glee and ride in fantasising about the warm shower and the tea and toast we were about to have.

But we'd soon become bored. Life was always elsewhere, in the forests and up the beaches and creeks. The city was just a moment of rescue.

Palm Island

— Patrick —

14 August 2014 to 21 August 2014

I'd told him our story: a family on bikes slowly recording all the free foods found in eastern Australia – camping, fishing and foraging along the way.

'We'd like to come to the Bwgcolman Community School and give a presentation on what we've been doing and meet people on the island who could show us some of your local foods.'

'Yeah, that sounds OK. When were you thinking?'

'This week, if possible.'

'Oh, we can't do that. People who come to talk to the kids are booked in weeks or months ahead. We've already got a full schedule at the school this week.'

'Yes, I understand,' I lied, 'but we don't know where we'll be from day to day. That's part of the story we'd like to present.'

I could sense his indifferent shrug and impatience

to get back to the million and four things he needed to be doing as school principal.

'Thanks for your time, Jeff.'

I was calling from a park in Townsville looking out to sea. I walked over to where Zero, Woody and Meg were sitting with Diana, an old friend from down south, and her young kids. I was ready to give up. The previous day I had contacted the Palm Island Aboriginal Shire Council to seek permission for us to visit. Our details were taken and I was told someone would get back to us. I thought about how local councils in the south of the country work in terms of returning calls, so I wasn't that hopeful we'd hear back.

'How did you go?' asked Meg.

'Doesn't look good,' I replied. 'We needed to have contacted the school weeks ago.'

As I said this something made me turn around and walk back over to my quiet spot in the park. I had been reading *The Interrogative Mood* by Padgett Powell and his line, 'Is there anything you might do today that would distinguish you from just being a vessel of consumption and pollution with a proper presence in the herd?' made me call the council again.

I'm always nervous making formal calls. I was also sensitive not to be a pushy whitefella. Because of all this awkwardness I was suddenly busting to do a piss and looked around for a discreet place to go as the receptionist answered my call. This time I was put through to a woman called Bernadine and I explained to her our reason for wanting to come.

'Yes. You and your family should be able to visit Palm Island. We have accommodation in the council-run motel.'

'Oh, that's great.' My nerves abated and my bladder relaxed.

'For how long were you thinking?'

'That depends on the cost. Is there a place we can pitch our tents in the motel grounds?' I asked. 'We're on a really tight budget.'

Bernadine gave me her email address and asked me to put everything in writing. The reason for our stay, how long it was for and when we wanted to come. I hung up and got to work.

'We might just get there after all,' I said to Meg and Diana. 'I spoke to a lovely lady called Bernadine who said she'd call me back this afternoon.'

In my email I explained to the council we were on a self-funded, low-budget research trip and that we were particularly interested in learning more about bush tucker and traditional Aboriginal nutrition. Bernadine got back to me that afternoon with the news they could sponsor us for a week in the motel for the same rate as two nights' accommodation.

'My boss has requested you say something nice about Palm on your blog,' said Bernadine shyly.

'Absolutely,' I responded.

I was aware of the negative press about the community over the years, especially the oft-repeated quote from the 1999 *Guinness Book of Records* that had named Palm Island the most violent place on earth outside a combat zone. Only a few years later Mulrunji Doomadgee would be found dead in a police cell, his body so battered it looked like he'd been hit by a truck. The enraged community rioted in retaliation and burnt two police buildings down to the ground. Bernadine's comment felt more like a plea for cultural sensitivity than a request for an advertorial, and fitted well within a gift exchange that we'd tried to articulate in our 'Letter to elders'. Palm Island was only just open to the public, but those who were allowed to visit were filtered.

The history of Palm Island is one of injustice, pain, struggle and resilience. The original tribe, the Manbarra, were joined by Aboriginal people from all over Queensland who, about a hundred years ago, were rounded up, held for several years at Hull River before a cyclone destroyed that settlement and were subsequently dumped on Greater Palm Island as a penal settlement, much like Nauru and Manus Island are today. Some were from the desert, others were coastal; together they became the Bwgcolman, meaning people of many tribes.

We got off the ferry after a few hours of vomitous chugging across rough water and intermittent throwdowns of rain. When we arrived the sun was shining and the jetty was packed with family members greeting loved ones, a few white policemen looking for sly grog, and children playing and fishing in the radiant green water. It was a spectacular sight: a bay town shouldered by a forested range and everywhere were dogs, fenceless and free, hungry and flea-ridden.

We wheeled our heavy bikes off last, asked directions to the council offices and met Bernadine. A gentle spirit, warm and welcoming, she took us to the motel, asking about our journey on the way.

We were trailed by a pack of dogs, eager to see what we had to eat or check out Zero and his unusual smells. We could sense Zero's excitement and terror as the pack languorously followed him – he was so small compared to most of them. We were a little anxious ourselves; where we come from, packs of dogs don't get around like this.

For the first time in our nine months of travelling it felt like we'd stepped into another country. Suburban Australia, which had more or less sprawled all the way up the east coast with its neat impenetrable fences and clean roads, was nowhere to be found.

Horses were untethered. The chain-link fencing we saw about the town was more about keeping these large free-rangers out than domesticated animals in. People knew whose horse or dog belonged to whom, wherever they roamed. Later, in Cairns, we were to hear how the only time the people of Yarrabah rose up to riot was when some whitefella took it upon himself to impound the community's dogs. By suburban standards the dogs on Palm were in poor health, but they had what most who live in non-Indigenous communities do not – the freedom to roam, to stray, to commune, to while away the day where they choose.

An avenue of giant, shade-producing mango trees lined the street the motel was on, aptly named Mango Avenue. Thousands upon thousands of little fruits were developing. We were sad we would miss the harvest. Cluster figs grew everywhere, as did tropical almonds. We unpacked our bags, locked our bikes in the communal kitchen, as advised by Bernadine, and went for a long walk.

One of the first plants I noticed on Palm was fleabane, a hardy, Roundup-resistant weed that grows everywhere, from Melbourne footpaths to right up here in far-north Queensland. The plant had played an important role in bubonic Europe, ridding plague-carrying fleas from people's homes. While on Palm, Zero was to have many a fleabane bath in the futile attempt to rid him of the little critters. Pigs and goats also roamed freely.

We were not the only non-Indigenous people on the island. School teachers, nurses, doctors, the CEO of the council, police officers and other professional folk like Jeff the principal lived here. But we were probably the only tourists on the island at that time, and the locals were inquisitive. Being here with a dog and a baby made meeting people much easier, as it had in other parts of the country. Another conversation starter arose on our third day when the *Townsville Bulletin* published our story.

Each day we spent walking or bike-riding around the island, recording all the free food and medicine we found and those that people were catching or harvesting. We came across Cape gooseberries, bush cucumbers and the peanut tree, all for the first time. About half a kilometre from the motel on our fourth day, a local man, Ashley Boyd, came out of his home brandishing the newspaper article for us to sign. We got talking and asked him what his favourite local foods were. He told us about Curacoa, one of the smaller islands we could see from the town.

'Full of goats. Doing their thing. Every now and then we go shoot one for a feed.' He pointed to a small group of islands. 'The closest one. Noogoo,' he said in language.

My permaculture mind exploded. Something so simple, so clear that it doesn't appear as anything at all – Aboriginal farming practices. No caged animals, no fencing, no transported feed, no wages and no need for synthetic medicines. Just the land, and the animals upon it in relationship with one another. The animals thrive on the plant life and the plant life thrives on the animals' waste. Populations are kept in check so there's no overgrazing. Humans behaving as apex animals, not superior gods.

Most of we newcomers have struggled to see Aboriginal food production as anything but chancy hunting and gathering, and their economics as simplistic and unformed. But what blindness! From ingenious eel traps to fire-stick farming of perennial grasslands and the invisible wallaby traps made with burning techniques, to an island full of autonomous goats, the working day only needs to be a few hours. It was simple, clear and appeared like nothing at all was going on.

When I was doing my masters degree in Sydney, one of the casual jobs my sister Hen arranged for me was cleaning offices with a group of visa-less young Iraqi men. We cleaned all over the city after hours, including for stockbrokers. In those buildings, at least at that time of day, it was mostly men playing office cricket, seven storeys high, with a rolled-up newspaper for a bat and a ball of scrunched up paper bound in masking tape. If they weren't playing cricket they were presumably moving around fleeting, abstract figures, divorced from the capacity of the land, the climate, rivers and oceans.

I looked out across to Noogoo and wondered how we might get over there. Food there wasn't under lock and key, you just needed a boat. Despite the constant indoctrination over the past century, a refusal to assimilate was pronounced on Palm. Even the town's clock tower was eternally set to the wrong time.

Nick was another Bwgcolman man who shared his knowledge with us. On our fifth afternoon he led us into the forest above the town to look for a particular medicine plant. Emu berries were out in fruit.

'Fruits are mashed and boiled,' he told us, 'makes a brew that treats diarrhoea, colds and flu. Also used for sore eyes.'

For Ashley, his favourite foods included fish and oysters, mangrove snails, crayfish and clams. He told us that just two dogs and a large knife are all that's needed to hunt wild boar.

While on Palm I received notice that my abstract for a paper on walked-for food and medicine had been accepted for a conference on Indigenous men's health in Cairns later in the year. I decided fairly quickly to focus the attention of the paper on what we were learning on Palm. Going to the conference, however, meant that we'd be locked into a deadline of being in one place at a particular time. We'd had the deadline of Christmas in Moss Vale and then later getting Zeph to Coffs airport. I wasn't sure I wanted to commit.

'You can always just get on a bus,' said Meg. 'We'll be up here somewhere still in October. I think it's really important you write this paper and go to the conference.'

The other thing that concerned me was the conference fee. All the other delegates would have their employers or universities pay the cost of $550. This independent researcher didn't have that kind of cash. No institutional status, no money, no fixed address.

But this is an asset, I convinced myself. In order to get gift economies back into use in everyday life we have to practise them. I wrote to the organisers explaining my situation and offered my skills as a facilitator of sessions, tech-guy (dubious), morning-tea waiter, anything in lieu of the fee. They wrote back with an invitation to be a guest speaker and waived all the costs. They liked the abstract for my paper and asked in return that I facilitate some breakout sessions. I was elated.

In the late afternoons we'd wander down through the streets with our hand lines and fish on the jetty with the local kids. We jagged barracuda and on a number of the nights we went back to the kitchen and made a broth with these bony fighter fish, or cooked them in a pan with trevally and queenfish. On other occasions we came across kids breaking open coconuts with rocks, taking it in turns to throw down the killer hit that would open up the white fleshy treat inside. The coconut shell was discarded, decomposing to become next year's nutrients. Also discarded throughout the island was plastic food and drink packaging, not unlike the rest of the country, but it stood out more in paradise.

'Look, Woody's found a bag and is picking up rubbish,' laughed Meg.

It was something he'd become accustomed to doing with his parents in each camp we made home, but this was the first time he did it of his own accord.

'For three million years human waste has been biodegradable and regenerative. It is only in the last few generations that it's become toxic,' I said. 'In the scheme of things what Woody's doing is actually ridiculous.'

'True,' said Meg. 'It would be like him picking up leaf litter because it's messy.'

'Yeah, that's called suburbia.'

We laughed. No wonder Zeph calls us hippies. His Ballarat grandparents sport a small strip of astroturf as their backyard lawn. You can actually vacuum it.

On the jetty one afternoon we met 20-year-old Wayne, fishing for dinner like us. His knowledge of traditional foods and medicines was exceptional. As we walked home with him, his partner Katrina and their newborn son, Wayne junior, we ran through a list of free foods, medicines and other useful species we had observed or consumed on the island. The medical records on Palm showed disproportionate rates of food-related illnesses such as type 2 diabetes and obesity, but did not tell the story of those families who were active and knowledgeable in getting their food. Neither did the reports discuss preventative measures. After speaking to John Rallings, the acting director of the Joyce Palmer health service on the island, it was clear that those families, albeit small in number, who were living on a more traditional diet were not of much interest, let alone an example, for the political class on the mainland that directed health funds.

'Western medicine is rarely about prevention,' John lamented when I visited him in his office. 'All the money today is invested in pharmaceutical companies or technology such as renal dialysis units. It's never about the cause.'

I brought up the island store with him, the only one on Palm. This mini-supermarket was owned by the Queensland government and for the first time in my life I saw 4-kilogram buckets of white sugar being sold.

'It's unbelievable, isn't it?' he said.

On the remote eastern side of the island where we had ridden one morning, we watched a teenager spearing for mullet. As he walked closer we could see he had a handmade three-pronged fishing spear. Such a beautiful tool doesn't just appear with the click of a mouse, like my hand spear had come to me. He was watching the light on top of the shallow water, looking for flashes that would indicate a school of almost completely camouflaged mullet. This was his school. I asked if I could photograph his spear.

'Yeah, me uncle taught me to make it.'

'Wow, beautiful,' said Meg. 'See the spear, Woody?'

Again, it appeared to be very simple. The prongs were modelled out of old car upholstery wire and the shaft was perfectly weighted to his height and arm extension. We talked for a little while but he was shy and keen to get going. He wore a small backpack and told me he was hoping to fill it with crabs and mullet. You couldn't assess this sort of learning, let alone standardise it. It was expansive, relational and autarkic, and exactly the kind of education Meg and I wanted for our boys.

After he'd left the beach and clambered up over the rocky bushland to the next beach, I mimicked his hunting style with my hand spear. I looked for the light and threw again and again, but it wasn't until our home stretch on the south coast of New South Wales that I'd spear my first mullet this way.

While on Palm, Meg and I thought about the disparity in skills between local kids here and those back home. We considered ways non-Indigenous kids could 'close the gap' on their knowledge of free-ranging, foraging, fishing, hunting and general life resilience that has disappeared from suburbia in just one or two generations. Helicopter parenting and passive consumption were doing little for young people, which we understood more significantly since coming to Palm Island.

On the way back from the beach, we came across a billabong loaded with the aquatic fern, nardoo. We photographed it but as there were no sporocarps to harvest we didn't get to taste this well-known bush tucker, which was supposed to have poisoned the explorers Burke and Wills. One theory is they didn't soak the sporocarps and pound the dried spores into a flour and cook them as a dense cake since they didn't have the local knowledge. Doing so would have removed the toxic enzyme thiaminase that kills thiamine in the body.

Referring to his painting of two echidnas hunting ants, reproduced as the cover art of the *Palm Island Health Action Plan 2010–2015,* Allan Palm Island, a traditional custodian and artist, wrote that echidnas are 'one of the traditional foods and like all bush tucker has a strong connection to the health and wellbeing of people on Palm Island'.

Was there a clearer statement about health? But eating echidnas for Aboriginal people doesn't involve money, so there's no inroad for other people to interfere. I remember speaking with an Aboriginal childcare worker in Redfern in 2010 about this and she said numerous people in Redfern would like to return to their ancestral land if the rivers weren't so impoverished and they had access to them to fish and camp.

With the help of the locals we counted over 60 species of beneficial flora and fauna on Palm. Made up of both traditional foods and newcomer species, no money is required to obtain these foods and medicines: mango, Chinee apple, banana, bush banana, African tulip tree, bush lemon, amaranth, coconut, barracuda, barramundi cod, sea turtle, bush passionfruit, snakeweed, snapper, trevally, brush turkey, echidna, beach calophyllum, possum, Burdekin plum, bush cucumber, cluster fig, goat, queenfish, clam, native mulberry, rock wallaby, mud mussel, spider shell, various crabs, pipi, cassava, sweet potato, naturalised squash (via horse droppings), mangrove snail, mud whelk, stingray, sea caper, beach cherry, pig, jackfruit, emu berry, Pacific rosewood, lady apple, fleabane, goats foot vine, dugong, grasshopper, naturalised tomato (again via horse droppings), green ant, guava, mullet, nardoo, native gooseberry, native rock fig, pandanus, pawpaw, peanut (or monkey nut) tree, mackerel, purslane, oyster and tropical almond.

This cursory list could be easily expanded with thorough research and further compilations of local food knowledges. A few crops such as taro and sweet potato could be grown to supplement this healthy pharmacopeia, and many of the plant species could be grown in food forest polycultures dotted around the main settlements.

Mandawuy Yunupingu, the rocker, elder and first Aboriginal school principal in Australia, developed a series of teaching methods culturally appropriate for the people of north-east Arnhem Land. He recognised that if you take away language, dance, song and food, then very little is left of a culture. At the Bwgcolman Community School we discovered boys are taught traditional dances and fire-stick farming methods, and evidence of such sensitive burning techniques could be seen all around the island. We witnessed numerous small burns, aimed at reducing fuel load in the forests while expanding more fodder for free-ranging animals. This gentle swinging between forest and diverse grassland was not aggressive like modern western agriculture, which bulldozes, fences, poisons, over-grazes and maintains complete control of a few grass species.

On the last night of our stay I was invited to the Bwgcolman Men's Group to talk about what we had been doing on the island. A male nurse from the health centre was also invited to speak. He had been working on the island for over two decades and because he wasn't a fly-in, fly-out white guy, he was more trusted by the community. His topic for the night was the sensitive issue of bowel cancer that most men, including myself, don't really want to think of, let alone talk about.

'Well, Patrick,' said one of the men, 'we've been seeing you and your family round Palm for the past week, and we'd like to know what you've been doing here.'

I liked his directness. I stood up.

'G'day. Thanks for inviting me along. My family and I are community gardeners and local food advocates travelling Australia by bicycle. We started down near Melbourne where we live, and we've been slowly crawling up the coast over the past nine months, camping and living pretty rough, making a list of all the free foods there are to eat in Australia.

'We're particularly interested in bush tuckers and we've come to Palm to learn more about the food and medicine you mob have here that you don't have to purchase. It could only have been one of my mob to come up with the stupid idea of paying for food.'

The room murmured chuckles of recognition.

'The question for my family and I is how to recreate your old people's lean logic, and we reckon the answer is to listen and learn from you mob; to hear the stories of your old people, the ones you care to share. Because they knew things about the land and about life that we need to understand again.'

I sat back down in my chair. There was a moment of awkwardness. Some of the men had only come because of the free feed at the end of the discussion, not to listen to a highfalutin blow-in. I'd spoken to a guy called Robert before the meeting and he said he hadn't eaten for two days. This wasn't the 'lean' I was referring to, but in light of Robert's immediate needs my position smacked of privilege. He'd told me he wanted to get into hunting, though conceded the knowledge was never handed down to him.

We all shared a meal of chicken and rice, and talked more about the food from the store in light of the food on the end of the spear.

After eight days on Palm I felt an overwhelming sense of gratitude to the people who showed us their island and shared their fruits. It was only a little porthole into life here, and we felt we could easily return and pick up the work we'd started.

But was this OK? Did the Bwgcolman people really need more whitefellas? It felt like worthwhile work we were doing, but what did the locals really think about it? Perhaps our political agenda of free food and gift economies was just quaint romantic idealism. I felt what we were learning from Indigenous people on this trip was profound, but I hadn't considered, until now, that perhaps this was just a one-way street.

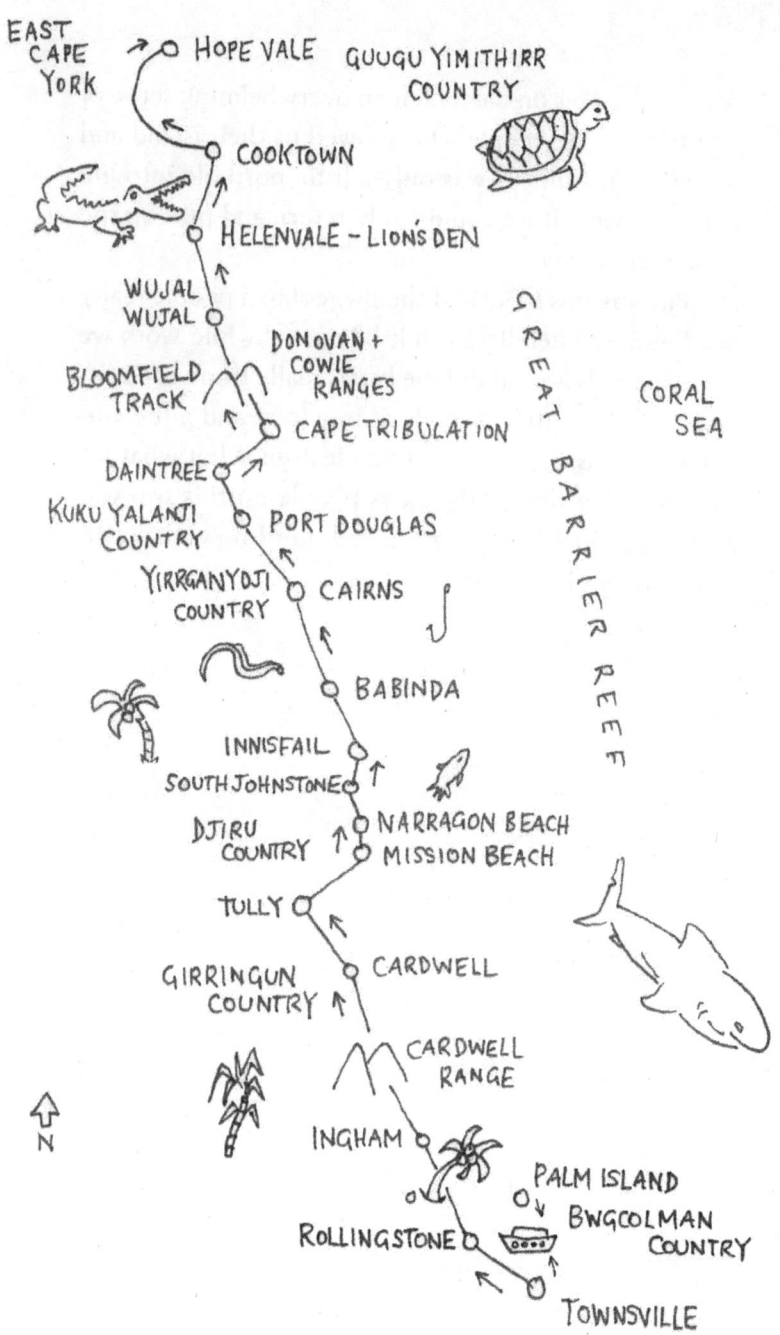

Opening out

– Meg –

PALM ISLAND to HOPE VALE
1000 KILOMETRES
21 August 2014 to 23 September 2014

'Not your teeth,' I said looking down at Woody. My nipple was on fire. Every time I plucked it from his mouth he would howl, so it was easier just to let him gnaw on it. Seized by seasickness, he glanced up at me then closed his eyes again. I leant back on the hard ferry chair and closed my eyes too, awaiting our arrival in Townsville.

We had had a remarkable week on Palm Island and I was sorry to leave. I was especially sorry for Woody, who I felt would be missing out if he lived anywhere else. Everywhere we went kids were outside – on the jetty, on the beaches, on the football fields, in the streets – the spirit of the island was one of play. Even though Patrick and I practise what's called idle parenting, whose maxim in relation to children is 'Leave them alone', I still had the unnerving feeling that after a while and despite ourselves we would be swept up into the mainland culture of over-scheduling, over-indulging and over-protecting Woody.

From when I was aged three to five my family lived on a kibbutz near Jerusalem. I saw my parents once a day, but otherwise I played and ate and slept with all the other kids on the kibbutz my own age. It was hard for my younger sister Emily, but for Kate, who lived with the bigger kids, and for me, it was formative; a time of joyous connection like a slumber party every night. Although we had carers, the way us kids free-ranged and looked after ourselves and each other reminded me of the kids on Palm. I wanted Woody to grow up with a similar experience.

Our next commitment was in October, when we had to be in Cairns for Patrick's conference. We arranged with Mel for Zeph to meet us there. We didn't know where we were going to be up until that time; we thought we might get as far north as Cape Tribulation.

We camped that first night off the island in a public park at Bushland Beach, 24 kilometres north of Townsville. We waited until dusk, until all the families eating fish and chips had gone home, then set up our tents. Snug in our sleeping bags, Woody and Zero asleep and Patrick working on his conference paper, I lay there thinking about our week on the island.

Who was it who said freedom, or the idea of liberty, is found mostly in hindsight? For us it was found on the

Opening out

days we didn't need to use money, in the closeness we felt with strangers, in the spirit of being new each day, in the simplicity of finding our own food, in belonging to the land. Not once did I ever wonder how I was going to integrate specific encounters and learnings into my being and my worldview. Until Palm.

Palm Island was the first time I'd had any meaningful interaction with an Aboriginal community. I felt like a child sitting at the feet of an entire culture. There was a looseness and un-preciousness that was invigorating and freeing. There were no self-conscious hipsters, no neatness, no overly controlled environments and little status anxiety. This was immensely powerful, and begged another way of being.

We rode back into sugar country as we approached Ingham, 112 kilometres north of Townsville. It had been such a relief to have a break from it, even though Woody and I loved singing our sugarcane song. Woody also loved singing 'Happy Birthday', though he had long forgotten the people we called at home to sing it to. This time it was his birthday, on 26 August. He was turning two, and Patrick – he was turning 44. I call them the 26-ers.

At the Info Centre in Ingham we enquired about staying at the council's free campsite, but were told it was only for RVs and caravans that had their own toilets.

'Then could you please tell us where the free camping is for non-polluters?' Patrick politely asked.

'Oh. I don't think we have any,' came the unsure reply.

We booked into a nearby caravan park where we celebrated the birthdays by showering, washing our clothes, pitching our tents on flat, watered, spongy lawn and cooking dinner in the communal kitchen that had a chopping board! Strainer! Pots!

Every so often it was restorative to have the few luxuries a caravan park provided. But I also felt this was a weakness, that I wasn't tough enough, that I was getting soft. At the same time, when we knew in advance where we were going to stay for the next few nights, if people had invited us to stay in their homes or if we knew ahead of time about free camping grounds, the thrill we felt finding an appropriate site and sleeping rough felt denied to us, that we had been robbed of the opportunity to court chance.

On the Cassowary Coast, 88 kilometres south of Cairns, we found blue quandongs. It was the first time we'd ever seen or tasted these sour, zingy blue fruits the size of large marbles. Not only were they appealing to look at – the blue was a shiny, radiant cobalt – they're also rich in antioxidants, vitamin E, folate, magnesium, zinc, calcium and iron, and are a favourite fruit of the majestic cassowary. And of Woody's.

Everywhere we went in this part of Queensland, we found more and more freely growing food. It was thrilling to be so far out of our climate zone (where much of the autonomous foods were either agricultural weeds or garden escapees), but we were fast becoming familiar with so many new species (mostly traditional Aboriginal bushfoods). Woody's favourite book was Les Hiddins' pocket-sized *Bush Tucker Field Guide*, which he'd pore over, calling out the names of the foods he recognised, and asking us to read the ones he didn't.

'What's this one, dada?'

'That's Tropical Almond. Remember we ate them on Palm Island?'

'It's a Twopicoo Armon,' Woody said to Lavina, a young elder of the Djiru tribe who was fishing with her man Hola.

It was a hot clear-skied day, the water a calm dark blue. We were fishing on Clump Point jetty, a few kilometres north of Mission Beach. The dozen or so other people fishing on the jetty that day all had serious rods and tackle boxes, but Hola and Lavina, like us, just had hand reels and a knife.

'Tox-ick!' Woody called out, showing Lavina the entry in the book with a red skull and crossbone in the corner.

'It's Cunjevoi,' Lavina said, 'and you're right, it is toxic if it's not prepared properly.'

I felt like a proud soccer mum as Woody flicked through the book reeling off all the names of the plants he knew. Later, we asked Lavina's permission to camp on her people's country, and after hearing our story — our research, travel and intentions — she encouragingly agreed.

Just north of the jetty we found a beautiful spot on Narragon Beach where we were able to tuck our bikes and tents into the undergrowth of the rainforest. We were happy to defy the local authorities if they tried to move us on, now we had Lavina's blessing, but at the same time we didn't set up camp to court conflict. We made a discreet home: a tarped-over bikeport, washing line and two tents, which soon expanded to three when once again Tom and our paths crossed.

The nearby town of Mission Beach was not too touristy, but large enough to warrant a small, well-stocked health-food store. And our campsite offered a lagoon of pure freshwater where we washed and swam, beside which we made our camp kitchen. We found fallen coconuts and firewood, and fished off the jetty where we caught yellowfin trevally, queenfish, jewfish and herring, which we cooked on our small beach fire. By now cooking on coals had become our preferred method, and we struggled to go back to using public barbecues after experiencing smoky, coal-kissed flesh.

'Ooh, breakfast in bed,' I whispered to Patrick one morning. He had just unzipped our tent and pushed through a fold-up bucket full of fish to show me. He had woken before dawn and walked down to the jetty where the fish were snapping madly for their breakfast. Woody was still asleep.

'This place is paradise,' he whispered back.

And it was. We had everything we needed: food, fresh water and an ideal campsite. But after a week of doing little else besides eating fish and coconuts, skinny-dipping, riding and walking, our pedals started itching again.

Opening out

'I feel it too,' I said to Patrick. He was boiling water in the billy on the small fire that I was collecting driftwood to feed. Woody was squealing as he chased Zero up and down the shallow lagoon.

'It's so weird,' Patrick said, stoking the coals as I dumped another load of wood onto the pile. 'What are we hoping to find at the next campsite that we don't have here?'

'I know. This really is a utopia.'

We were both watching Tom, about 20 metres away, tying a piece of heavy-duty elastic around his ankles at the base of a coconut palm, then practising his climbing technique. He moved himself up the tree, shimmying his legs, the tight elastic holding his weight after each lunge.

'But is this trip about finding the most idyllic spot and staying put?'

We left reluctantly the next morning after a swim and a slow pack-up. We had ridden every day over the last week, but only short trips, and now, with my bike fully loaded, my legs felt empty of strength. My restored senses immediately went into shock after we got back on the Bruce. Trucks, cars, obscenely large 4WDs, buses, motorhomes, caravans, roadside memorials, endless roadkill – kangaroos, possums, eastern grass owls, snakes, quolls, rabbits, wombats – discarded food and drink packaging and sugarcane, sugarcane, sugarcane. We found a backroad to Innisfail via South Johnstone and Japoon. It was longer, but we were happy to cruise along, especially after we came across a river to swim in and a grove of oranges and passionfruit. We approached the farmer to see if we could harvest some.

'My mother planted them years back. Go ahead, take as many as you can carry. No one eats them anymore.'

At the free camp ground by the river in Babinda, Patrick hand-speared a small black fish for bait and on our 40-pound hand line caught an Australian long-finned eel that was as thick as my fist and just over a metre long. He wrestled with it for some time, with Woody and I cheering him on, before he was able to bring it onto the bank. This powerful creature was heavenly eating after cooking on the coals, 12 minutes each side, and peeling back the bitter skin to reveal the extraordinary white, moist flesh that tasted a little like chicken. There was so much meat, we were more than happy to share it with our neighbours who had gathered around our fire to swap what information they had about a fellow camper who'd had a heart attack in his RV that afternoon, and was recovering in hospital in Cairns.

Cairns marked the end of the Road of Death that spilled into the outer industrial sprawl of the metropolis, its beautiful coastline screened by urban development. Like most Australian cities, Cairns was a big car-centric shopping centre. Apart from finding a great food co-op where we stocked up, we also raided the op-shops for some clothing. After ten months on the road, it was really telling which of the gear we had was made well and what was cheap rubbish. Seams were starting to come undone, zips were jamming, hems were peeling away and sleeves were fraying. Our German-made bicycle panniers, however, seemed invincible. We took my boots to a repair place to have their zips fixed, but I ending up buying a new pair as it would have cost more to repair than what I'd paid for them. People often remarked on our work boots and wondered why we didn't wear clip-in cycling shoes. Simple: boots can be worn on the bike, through the scrub, up trees as well as in town. Cycling shoes have one use only, and never made our equipment list.

As we reached northern Queensland we started observing green tree ants everywhere, in parks, gardens and in the bush. They weave their incredible nests with leaves, in trees, suspended some distance above the ground. Because of their high fat content, they are perfect as cycling fuel. They are zingy and sweet, which is not surprising as they love all kinds of fruit, especially citrus. We all learnt to catch the ants by the head in a pincer squeeze, killing them instantly and popping them whole into our mouths. Woody particularly enjoyed chasing and gobbling them. It was his first form of hunting.

Not far north of Port Douglas we met Simon and Alia, a cycle-touring couple from Sydney. Where many cyclists may avoid or dread hills, this dynamic duo were seeking them out as part of a project they were working on called the Great Dividing Range Bicycle Touring Route. We felt a closeness with them and their adventurousness. After sharing some notes about the Bloomfield Track, which they had just been on and which we were considering tackling, we shared some grapefruit we'd found on a nearby tree, and pedalled on to Newell Beach. A large croc was sighted there the day before, so we sought haven in the local caravan park instead of a stealthy site along the beach.

The grapefruit, we discovered that night, were full of Queensland fruit-fly maggots. I braved up and munched down on these squishy citrus-infused lil wrigglers.

'They're not as bad as you think,' I said, chewing firmly, though I was in no hurry to take another bite. Patrick was both appalled and impressed, but just couldn't bring himself to join me.

Prone to regular flooding and constant change, the Daintree River was abuzz with life. We paid to go out on a boat with a guide who pointed out things our eyes were unaccustomed to: a grand male estuarine crocodile, and common tree snakes sunning themselves. We also learned about taro, which some think of as a newcomer weed from tropical Asia, though it's unclear how long the plant has been in Australia. From Linda, a Kuku Yalanji elder, we learned how to harvest freshwater mussels while keeping a vigilant eye out for crocs. We also heard from Linda that there were many significant Aboriginal places surrounding the village, including a burial site that she said the local historical society wasn't interested in marking.

Opening out

I was looking forward to arriving in the Daintree. My folks had visited there when I was younger and their photos of lush rainforest thick with moss-covered trees, vines and ferns, unusually coloured birds and the serpentine river had stayed in my mind all these years.

It didn't disappoint. But we also found a complex mix of attitudes and industries that were anything but idyllic. Farmers let their cows shit in the river, racism was present and great tracts of sugarcane abutted the park. We'd photographed piles of empty chemical containers on nearby banana plantations. After researching it, we learned that the pesticide, Gramoxone 250, is banned in 32 countries, including China and the EU.

We explored the small village by bike and went on some long walks in the surrounding dense rainforest, but mostly we rested and mentally prepared for the Bloomfield Track, which by now we had decided to ride, then go as far as Cooktown. We knew we were nearing our most northerly point and wanted to test our resilience, resolve and endurance before we turned for home.

The day we left, a small crowd gathered to photograph and cheer us as we set off towards Cape Tribulation, 48 kilometres away. We camped a night at Diwan and then it was on to the Bloomfield:

CAUTION
BLOOMFIELD ROAD
PAST CAPE TRIBULATION
SLIPPERY, BOGGY
CONDITIONS
4WD ONLY

'Are you sure you want to do this?' I asked Patrick. I could see he was up for it but I was shitting myself.

'Beep, beep, beep,' I said, imitating a reversing truck.

'It'll be short and painful this way,' he said. 'If we go inland, it means hundreds of kilometres more riding, and we have to come back that way. If we go this way we won't have to backtrack.'

Even though I had faced my fear of riding on gravel on the way to Marlborough, from all accounts this track was in a category of its own. It traversed two mountain ranges, and in parts was so steep some 4WDs weren't able to make it through. Built in the face of protests in the early 1980s, the roadworks minimised the damage to the forest by placing as few switchbacks and bends as possible, creating gradients of up to 33 per cent.

Thirty-three! The most we had walked with our bikes, let alone ridden up, was 20. What with a baby and ridiculously heavy panniers I didn't think we were going to make it.

'You go ahead,' I called out. 'Woody and I are going to ride back to Cairns. We'll meet you in a few weeks.'

'Meg!' he said sternly. 'You are one of the toughest women I know. You are capable and strong. You've even eaten fucking maggots! You can do this!'

'I can't,' I said shaking my head, feeling close to tears. 'It's not that I won't. I honestly can't.'

'Don't be stupid!' he said, riding off, leaving me there.

I wasn't being stupid. I had slipped over too many times on gravel and had taught my young son too many swear words in the process.

And I had cried and cried when we nearly ran out of water on the way to Marlborough.

But I also got up. I stopped crying. We found water. I felt strong and regretted nothing. I took a big breath through my nose and exhaled loudly through my mouth.

'OK,' I whispered to Woody as I pushed off. 'Here we go.'

Have you ever noticed that photographs always flatten the picture plane, making steep inclines look almost horizontal? The photos we took that afternoon look almost comical. There I am, brown with caked-on dust, grimacing as I push my bike up another killer hill that looks as flat as a cricket pitch. But the photos lied. The inclines were almost vertical and I wasn't walking my bike at all. I hadn't been able to. I was standing beside it, gripping my brakes for dear life. My knuckles were so white I thought my bones would poke through my skin. If I let go even a little bit to relieve the pressure, my bike started to slide downhill on the loose rocks.

'Careful Imma!' became Woody's mantra.

Patrick laughed the first few times he pushed his bike to the top of a hill, found a resting spot to lean it, then ran down to help me up with mine, while I pushed from behind. But after the sixth or seventh time, the joke was well and truly over.

We entered a kind of time warp as we huffed and puffed and shluffed up and down the Donovan, then Cowie, Ranges, 4WDs fanging past, causing dust to swirl up and make its way into every possible nook. Sometime before dusk, the dying light indicated that we should call it a day. We rode on for another hour before we found an appropriate site, ten metres off the road next to the shell of a smashed-up car. Patrick put up the tents and I made a crude dinner of pita bread and limp salad by torchlight.

'How much further do you think we have to ride tomorrow?' I asked Patrick when we were finally in bed.

'We rode six hours today,' he said. 'The track's 30 kilometres long. I have no idea.'

One or two more cars raced by, then either no more passed or I passed out.

The following morning Patrick woke up with a sore back and aching knees. I felt fine, but then I had only climbed each hill once.

We weren't expecting a ticker-tape parade, but we were expecting to reach the end of the track at the bottom of the next hill, around the next bend, after the next river crossing, just beyond that big hollow tree, just past the road workers building a new bridge, shortly after that 4WD adventure bus went by, on the other side of the next monstrous climb, no, this one, *definitely*. We no longer had fresh muscles. We struggled with the heat, the dust, the flies, our thirst and 4WDs zooming by like we weren't even there.

And then we arrived, crossing over a newly built bridge into the quiet Aboriginal town of Wujal Wujal, a collection of 100 or so houses dotted around the main road and into the surrounding bush, to not quite a parade, but a cheering group of tourists who were on the adventure bus that passed us on the track. From their air-conditioned, padded-seat hotel on wheels, we were like curiosities in a travelling circus. We parked our dust-covered bikes and were handed a cup of tea by one of the tour guides, then sweet biscuits.

I found a rock a little way from the gathering and sat down to breastfeed Woody. I rode over the Bloomfield Track, I thought to myself, practising how it might feel to remember this in the face of future adversities, to remind myself of my resilience when we returned home, but I couldn't for the life of me think of a single situation at home where I might have to use it.

At the Bana Yirriji Art and Cultural Centre we met community elder Sharon Walker, who suggested we ride the few kilometres to the Bloomfield Falls, a sacred site for the community.

'In our local language,' Sharon told us, 'Wujal Wujal means many falls.'

We spent the afternoon washing, cooking, napping, fishing and swimming in this oasis, disbelieving the contrast of our previous 24 hours on the hot, dangerous and waterless Track.

The following morning we pushed off into another hard day's ride, 40 gravelly, hilly and dusty kilometres to the famous watering hole, the Lion's Den Hotel, north of Helenvale. The Den offered a campground on the banks of the Little Annan River. We paid for a patch of ground, had our first warm shower in a while and were enjoying a quiet ale on the deck when we got talking to

Julie, or rather, I got talking. Patrick was beyond conversing; I'd never seen him so tired and after just one beer he'd reached a semi-comatose state, capable of only staring up towards the thousands of unripe mangoes in the hundred-year-old trees, smiling occasionally and nodding.

Julie had seen us earlier that day riding north of Wujal and immediately invited us to stay and rest with her family in Cooktown.

The next morning we rode a slow and achey 31 kilometres and explored the town that sat between the Coral Sea and Rinyirru National Park. The town's distance from Cairns seemed to act as a protective buffer from the typical far-north tourism we'd witnessed, making Cooktown, to us, more appealing. Tourism existed but didn't dominate like Port Douglas and the other schmaltzy towns we'd hightailed from. We found a jetty towards the end of the main drag where we spent the afternoon fishing. In Queensland, permits are not required, but size and catch limits apply.

'There is a redneckery here I love,' Patrick said, plopping his line into the water. 'Families can feed themselves for free without bureaucracy.'

We had loathed the incessant permits and laws in NSW, not that we acknowledged many of them. On the jetty that afternoon, a local guy told a tourist to throw back an undersized Spanish mackerel.

'That will be for my grandchildren,' we heard him say.

Patrick caught two of these magnificent creatures

Opening out

that afternoon to take as gifts to Julie and her husband Alistair and their kids. While Julie cooked them up for dinner, I made a big salad and helped set the table. When we were all seated and ready to eat I went outside to see what was taking Patrick so long.

'What's up?' I asked, walking towards him. 'Dinner's ready.'

'This fucking grass.' He was almost in tears. 'It's so hard and dry it spiked through the bottom of the tent and popped my sleeping mat. I've had to patch them.'

'Oh Jaysus!'

'I had to take the tent down, cut the grass with my knife, then put it up again over the folded tarp. It's all good now,' he smiled up at me, recognising it was no big thing.

'Oh Jonesy.'

I helped put the last of the panniers in the tents then we walked hand in hand to join the others.

This man, I thought to myself. This ridiculously amazing man. I squeezed his hand as hard as I could. I didn't feel like the luckiest person alive to have him in my life; luck didn't really come into it. It was more about timing and opportunity, chemistry and, sometimes, lots of hard work. But the love I felt for him was as easy as a tailwind. The day before, I had seen him at his very best; his hardiness blew my mind.

I had also seen him at his worst: he was foul-tempered and unreasonable and too hard on the world. Lots of people give a shit about things, but here was a man who acted. He was the toughest motherfucker I knew, with a tenderness that could bring me to tears. He was just and fair; he righted wrongs. And with him by my side, I felt expansive, monumental, a better version of myself.

We spent three nights with Julie and Alistair, perched high above Cooktown looking north over the water. Their girls Amber and Savannah spoiled Woody with hours of play, stories and dressing him up in their clothes. Amber taught us about the soap tree in their garden, how to crush the leaves with a little water to create an instant bush shampoo. Savannah showed us the broad-leaf native cherry with its edible red fruit, a relative of our needle-leafed native cherry back home.

We were desperate to keep pushing north. Would we ever travel this far up the continent again? We would have loved to have ridden to the very tip of Cape York Peninsula and, with permission, visited some of the Torres Strait Islands. But the tip was still 800 kilometres away along the unsealed Peninsular Development Road that boasted corrugations a foot deep, clouds of powdery dust and few places to refill water bottles. When a local man told us about the head-on collisions that happen on that road due to poor driving conditions we knew it was out of the question.

We thought we'd have just enough time to visit the Aboriginal community of Hope Vale, 40 kilometres north, then head south to be in Cairns in three weeks' time. I wasn't ready to head homewards yet, but the idea was certainly beginning to ripen in my mind. The thrill of the open road still beckoned.

Opening out

We left Cooktown, my feet pushing hard on the pedals, the word in time with my breath, north ... north ... north ...

Hope Vale

– Patrick –

23 September 14 to 1 October 2014

We pulled up in the main drag and I made a call while Meg put together a lunch of bread and hardboiled eggs under a large fig tree. As usual, we could have eaten a horse. Like Palm, there were a few floating around. Zero introduced himself to the local dogs.

'Your people have been here before us, Meg. Look, Poland Street,' I said, as the phone lit up.

'Hello, Patrick,' a man with a soft, grandfatherly voice spoke. 'Duncan says you need a place to stay.'

'Yes. Hello. Thanks for calling back. Yes, we do.'

I walked away from Woody, who was squealing noisily at Zero and another dog.

'You've ridden a long way,' said Tim McGreen, a Guugu Yimithirr elder.

Hope Vale

'Yes. If it's OK with you, we'd like to spend some time in Hope Vale.'

'That'd be allright. You can stay at my place. Where are you now?'

'That's great, Tim. Thank you. We're near the store, in Poland Street.'

'I'll come and get you now. I have a funeral to go to this afternoon.'

The day we arrived on Palm Island there was a funeral and we were advised to make ourselves scarce. I asked Tim whether we should do the same.

'The farm's 4 kilometres out of town,' he replied. 'You can stay there this afternoon.'

Before we met Duncan and his family in Cooktown we were going to head out to Hope Vale, visit the council and ask their permission to camp. But having arrived, we could sense that this may have been insensitive.

Duncan's work with Aboriginal lawyer and activist Noel Pearson's Cape York Partnership had enabled him to develop friendships in Hope Vale and his interest in our adventure meant that those connections were generously passed on. Tim later told us he had gone to school with Noel. They grew up on the same dusty streets with the European names – Kernich, Wenke, Keller, Kotzur, Flierl. From what we understood the Lutherans were strict. Neat yards and tidy appearances were everything, and this influence was still somewhat apparent in the town. Alcohol was the untidy response to these ideals.

'There's a big grog debate going on here,' said Tim, as he showed me where the generator was in the old shipping container on the farm.

He filled it up, primed the engine and pulled the cord. 'You can have a shower now and do some washing.'

'Thanks, Tim. Do you want us to cook you dinner when you get back?'

We didn't know if Tim lived alone or with family. There was no one else out on the farm apart from his dog, Jimbo the dingo.

'That'd be good, Patrick.'

After Tim left we unpacked, made up our beds in the spare room and walked down to the Endeavour River. We swam and let all the stresses of the road leak out into the cool water. I screwed my hand spear together and went off to see what I could catch for dinner. The river was fairly shallow in places, awaiting the coming wet season. Meg and Woody lay in the water naked, sunning themselves. Tim told us crocs wouldn't be so far upriver at this time of year. I moved through the water, propelling myself slowly forward by gently kicking, my testicles and penis hanging down, exposed to every creature the river homed. Visibility was not great. I imagined my unmarried wedding tackle being bitten off by a spiteful eel who'd heard about my exploits back at Babinda.

'I think we'll have pasta tonight,' I yelled down to Meg, standing up in shoulder-high water. 'How many packets have we got?' I moved to the shallows and walked towards her.

'Two ... Oh, hello stranger!' she replied, raising her eyebrows.

Hunting, even my continual failures, always piqued her interest.

We cooked dinner outside the house as the sun was closing for the day. We were weary and hungry and Tim still wasn't back.

'He may have eaten at the wake,' said Meg.

'Yeah, I reckon I'll just cook enough for us for now.'

We cleaned up, put the fire out and Meg was about to put Woody to bed when Jimbo stirred and Zero, in reaction, started barking.

'Head torch!' I snapped at Meg.

I shone it on the ground near where Jimbo had been lying. A small snake writhed its way under the table we'd used to prepare the pasta. I couldn't tell which kind. Luckily Zero ran off barking in another direction. I flashed the light around to see whether there was an angry parent about. The torch landed on another noteworthy critter, a scorpion with its tail erect, moving around just near Woody's bare feet.

'Right, bedtime,' said Meg clutching him up.

'Good night, little traveller,' I kissed Woody on the nose, torched a path for them to walk back to the house, then returned to the snakes and scorpions and packed up the food pannier.

Quite suddenly, like down in the river, life was dangerous again, only it was dark now, and I was hanging out with a dingo I hadn't yet built a rapport with.

The house was a kit home built through a loan

scheme Noel and Duncan had helped set up. We'd turned the generator off hours earlier and didn't want to spark it up again just for lighting. I liked that there was no glass. The large openings had either rolling or hinged shutters, and all manner of critters could move freely in and out.

After about twenty minutes I tiptoed into the bedroom to see if Woody was asleep. Everyone was: Zero curled at the base of Woody's mattress, Meg in her usual spot on the right side of our bed. I was concerned I hadn't asked Tim whether it was OK for Zero to be in the house. I was also concerned about Tim's dinner. He's probably eaten, I thought, but I'll read for a bit and wait up for him, just in case he hasn't.

The next thing I heard was Zero barking. I must have fallen asleep, my head torch was still on and my book in my hands. A vehicle was coming through the bush. Jimbo didn't bark, a good sign I thought, he must have recognised it as Tim's. I wondered whether I should stay in bed. Then I worried again about the dinner I had promised to make. I got up.

'Zero! No!' I growled to stop him barking.

I noticed two people getting out of the car. A woman. This must be Tim's wife. They seemed sombre. The funeral? Perhaps they'd had an argument? About us being here?

'Hello, Tim,' I said coming into the kitchen. 'Are you still wanting dinner?'

'Yes,' he answered, like it was a stupid question.

'We didn't cook extra because we didn't know when

you'd be home. I'll cook some up now,' I said, awkwardly.

'Hello, I'm Patrick. Would you like some too?' I addressed the woman who was attending to the laundry.

'I'm Elaine,' she said, turning towards me. A warm smile spread across her face that immediately put me at ease. 'You've been on a big trip.'

I got the fire going. The water eventually boiled in the billy. Tim had fired up the generator and set up some better lighting that made cooking outside a little less terrifying. I chopped up ginger and garlic and added it raw to the cooked spelt pasta which I dressed with olive oil and salt. I stirred it all through with a spritz of lemon and hoped they'd like it.

'This is what we eat when we don't catch anything,' I said. 'I had a fish in the river today, but no luck.'

'This is lovely,' said Elaine, then added, 'Zaymon caught a big fish down there a few days ago.'

Elaine's voice was gentle and calming. 'Zaymon, Tristian and Irie will probably come over tomorrow. You'll meet them. They're my grandchildren.'

'We're going to my father's country on the weekend,' said Tim. 'Would you mind looking after the farm for us, Patrick?'

'Yes, sure,' I said, feeling more comfortable. We had a role now, or at least a way of contributing.

'Then next Tuesday is Men's Group, I'd like you to come along.'

'Great. I'd love that, Tim.'

'There's a number of people you need to meet while you're here.' He paused. 'We got to get on to that stuff you were talking about earlier. The health stuff. We've left it too long.'

He got up to go inside. He looked exhausted. Elaine followed while I cleaned up. She later told us Tim suffers from type 2 diabetes, like many in the community.

'You can let the generator run out, Patrick. It will heat water for the morning.'

Tim and Elaine's grandson Zaymon and his friend Muundhu came over the next day, keen to see our bikes. I rode them through the bush on the tandem, strung up the long bow and taught them how to draw and shoot an arrow, and in turn they took me down to the river and taught me their method of fishing.

'Hey Mister,' said Zaymon laughing, 'your spear's too long for diving this river.'

The boys were sharing a spear half the length, which enabled them to go into the little pools without it getting caught up in the branches and logs. Instead of gliding down or up the river as I would in deeper water hovering on the surface, looking down through goggles and breathing through a snorkel, the boys dived down into the pools with what they called their diving glasses, holding their breath. They'd wait and watch intently until they'd have to come back up for air. After not much time Zaymon rose to the surface excitedly.

'Jewfish, Mister, down there.'

Muundhu and I watched from above the water. We could see Zaymon on the hunt now, moving quickly under the surface and then saw his spear release, the rubber causing a shudder as it sent the tip fighting through the viscosity of the water into the fish.

'See, Mister,' said Zaymon proudly, holding the fish as though these two words were enough to say everything about his method. His technique was only subtly different from mine but startlingly more effective.

'Jewfish, Mister, biguthirr.'

Muundhu laughed at his friend, telling me the language name.

'Big-a-tur,' I tried to repeat, causing both boys to laugh.

'Biguthirr,' repeated Zaymon.

'Big-a-durr,' I struggled again, my ears not picking up the last syllable for my mouth to form.

The boys laughed again, and this time I joined them. If only Zeph were here, I thought, as we climbed the bank back up to the house, he'd be in boy-and-riverbank heaven. Zaymon and Muundhu were to be just two of a gang of boys ranging from eight to twelve years old that would sometimes ride with us as we travelled to town or back. For a brief moment we became the bikie gang of Hope Vale.

On one ride, heading into town, Zaymon came up alongside Meg's bike and extended his hand to Woody. Woody reciprocated and they travelled along the road holding hands and laughing. I rode behind watching, engulfed by a posse of boys cheering and calling out. I began to cry as I fumbled for my camera.

This is what reconciliation looks like, I thought. I

could see in my helmet mirror that no cars were coming. Nothing was going to spoil this unbridled moment. No helmets, no shoes, not enough bikes, boys being dinked on their mate's handlebars, one on the back of my tandem, which they took turns on and fought over who'd had more time than another.

We visited the Hope Vale Knowledge Centre and introduced ourselves to Dora Gibson, the senior librarian. Dora told us about the various community food-growing initiatives, including the community orchard a few kilometres out of town and asked us whether we wanted to see it.

Brazilian cherries, soursop and mulberries were in fruit, and as we walked around the 5-acre property with her, eating these fruits and talking about their ethnicity, I couldn't help think that if these trees were in town, in the streets, within walking distance to people's homes, they'd be more likely incorporated into the local diet. Kids would pass by and collect the fruit from the traditional food trees like noni fruit and nonda plums as well as exotics such as bananas, cashews, macadamias and mangoes as they moved from mates' homes to aunties' and uncles'. The town's foodstore was like Palm Island's. Those families who were not as affected by such an adverse western diet ate less from the store and more from the local land and nearby sea.

Outside the library Dora showed us her favourite local tree. She told us the fruit of the Great Morinda (noni, cheesefruit, or in language dugunyja) is juiced in the community to help treat diabetes.

Dora suggested I visit her brother Clarry. Meg and Woody headed back to the farm while I rode around and knocked on his door. A tall, slender man in his sixties greeted me warmly and made a cup of tea for us both. We chatted about our travels and our mutual interest in bush tucker and medicines. He told me to come back later in the week and he'd take me through a few brews.

When I got back to Tim and Elaine's farm, Meg was cooking dinner and talking to Elaine in the kitchen. Woody was outside with the dogs. A number of them had shown up now, but Jimbo was the pack leader. Woody was naked, walking Irie's bike around, or trying to work out how to manage it when it got bogged in the dust. He would get himself up, try to move it and fall over again.

'Look, Dada, Irie bike.'

All those thousands of kilometres singing and speaking with his Imma had produced a very expressive two-year old.

'I can see, Woody,' I replied.

'You see Dada, see Irie bike.' He was so pleased with himself.

'He's been out there for over an hour,' Meg said when I went inside.

The next day Tim and Elaine, the grandkids and numerous trucks of family members headed up to Tim's father's country at Jack River for the long weekend. They took the generator, several dogs, swags and mattresses and left us to the quiet of the farm. It was a chance to rest but we also needed some supplies. We decided to ride into town, leave our bikes at the home of Pastor David, who Tim had earlier introduced us to, and hitch into Cooktown.

Our trip was a bumpy, dusty roller-coaster ride with two old men who were going to meet a friend off the Cairns bus. Lewis, the driver, had marginal English. We had even less Guugu Yimithirr. There was lots of laughing, sliding across the gravel and bracing Woody and Zero as the four of us took up the back seat of a Suzuki 4WD. Lewis's driving was not reckless and we didn't feel unsafe, but the authorities down south in the affluent nanny states would have had a field day with their sirens and notebooks.

We caught the Cooktown Saturday market, stocked up on some local produce but just missed the newsagents, which closed at midday. I could see a copy of Noel Pearson's newly released *Quarterly Essay* staring at me from inside the locked doors. I imagined being busted for breaking in and stealing a copy, how I'd be the most literary crook in the far north.

We caught a lift back with a nurse from the health service. She told us she was related to Dora. We spoke about our research interests and she asked whether we'd been to see Old Pastor George.

'He has great knowledge on bush food and medicine,' she said. 'Only he's old now and fairly deaf. You should try to visit him at the old people's home.'

She dropped us outside Pastor David's, which was

next to the home. I went in to enquire when would be a good time to see Pastor George. The nurse on duty said I could see him now, so we collected our bikes and Meg took Woody back to the farm and I took Zero with me. I knocked on the old man's door and waited. I knocked again. The nurse came by and was less polite: BANG! BANG! BANG!

'Hey George, you have a visitor,' he said, barging in.

'Hello, George,' I added.

'You'll need to speak up,' said the nurse, 'he won't hear a thing.'

'G'day, George,' I shouted.

He looked up and squinted. I smiled. 'My name is Patrick. I'm interested in talking with you about bush medicine.'

I think we'd woken him and understandably he appeared a little put out. He put on his glasses and the nurse suggested we sit on the verandah. George told me he was 84 and that he grew up in a time when there were no hospitals.

'We never depended on them,' he said. 'We depended on bush medicine.'

George's people came from Laura, a community about 100 kilometres west. He spoke about three significant medicines that were commonly used when he was young. The first was dugong (girrbathi, munhaarri) oil, a traditional food-medicine that was also administered daily to the community by the strict but supposedly popular Lutheran pastor Schwartz. The second was green-ant (thinggan) juice to treat colds and flus, constipation and also used as a natural antiseptic. The third was fruit-bat (thulgu, thiibuul, jungginh, gaambi) soup, which was given to children for a range of health issues including colds, coughs and asthma, much like chicken soup in Jewish culinary culture.

'But today we're losing the knowledge,' he said flatly.

When Tim and Elaine returned after the long weekend they had a large feral boar on the back of their truck. It had already been gutted and Zaymon helped his grandfather clean it. They took it to a cousin to butcher and apportion it to family members.

'That's the idea,' said Tim laughing. 'But we may never see any.' He didn't seem concerned.

Tim told us about what happened on Saturday night at Jack River when all the children had settled down by the fire. The kids were quiet for the first time all day and as he spoke he noticed, on the ridge, the form of a wild pig. The stillness of storytime erupted into a wild hunt with children and dogs, men and women chasing and shouting. Jimbo returned with a deep gash above his eye – a mark of the pig's last stand.

The next day Tim drove me into town earlier than I needed to get to Clarry's because there was someone else he wanted me to meet. Neville Bowen, Dora and Clarry's brother, worked for the council and taught young men to make traditional tools and weapons. Neville showed me one of his fishing spears. It had been weighted to the reach of his arm, just like the teenager's on Palm. It was a deadly thing, beautifully made and required an ironwood babaar (woomera) to throw it.

'Do you mind if I photograph your spear and babaar?' I was getting used to the language.

'No, go ahead,' he said laughing.

I photographed him from different angles. It's hard to photograph something that's long and very narrow. I lay down in front of him and asked him to consider me prey. He laughed again as I clicked away with my crappy little point-n-shoot. He was fairly amused by my performance.

'I'm going to see your brother now. He's going to take me through his bark brews.'

'See that tree over there?' he replied. 'That's my medicine tree. Gundaar.'

'What's it good for?' I asked.

'Aw, toothache, blood pressure, broken bones. Lots of things.'

'Clarry told me that if a tree can heal itself then it's a medicine tree.'

'Yeah. That's right.'

'That makes sense,' I said.

Tim had had to go to a meeting. He'd said something about his signature being required for a mining company, so he left me to chat to Neville. Walking over to Clarry's I wondered about what Tim was signing. The streets I was walking were set out in a grid. The attempts to straighten out Guugu Yimithirr people with white food, religion, town planning and 'real' economics were everywhere to be seen, as were the failures.

Clarry greeted me and we bundled into his truck and headed out to see one of his trees. He wasn't entirely sure of its name, he just knew what it did. He chipped off the outer layer of bark and discarded it before chipping and collecting inner bark and putting some into a bag.

'Down south, Clarry, someone would manufacture a product like this bark medicine, wrap it in fancy packaging and ship it all over the world, advertising it to convince people they couldn't live without it.'

He chuckled and nodded. 'You're talking about bottled water,' he said.

We both laughed. I thought about the John Berger line, 'He who could buy courage was brave, even if he was a coward'.

We returned to his home where three children were playing outside. He asked them to help cut some bark from the big tree in the backyard, which he thought might be a very old Brazilian cherry.

'One rodeo time,' he told me, pointing to one of the children, 'this little guy broke out in hives, lumps everywhere. We were up at Laura ... came back home at four o'clock in the morning, and the poor kid was scratching himself, rolling around on the concrete, itchy. So six o'clock I got up, got my tomahawk and started cutting away ... boiled it up, made a big pot of juice ... I had to put him in the sink ... and bathed him in there with the juice ... Picked him up, never towelled him down or anything ... by lunchtime the lumps were all gone.'

I followed Clarry inside to the kitchen. He put the two different barks into separate pots, added water to both and turned on the stovetops. We chatted while the brews came to the boil. He told me each medicine cured a host of complaints, that the first one, like his brother's, was good for toothache and aching bones, while the tree in his backyard was not only good for ailments like hives and cancer recovery but was also his Viagra tree.

'I'd like to take some of this first one back to Meg.'

Breastfeeding Woody was giving her sore teeth, presumably because much of her body's calcium was going into milk production. We tried the second brew. The Brazilian Viagra one was fruitier and more pleasant to drink.

'Better not give this one to Meg,' said Clarry, chuckling, 'it may knock her up.'

'Oh no, we don't want that!'

If Clarry and I lived in the same community I was sure I'd be over at his place trying all sorts of brews and getting his opinion on various experiments.

'Perhaps you could come back next year, Patrick, and we could make that bush medicine film you were talking about.'

'I'd really like that, Clarry.'

Tim had organised to meet me at the Men's Shed that night for the meeting, so after saying goodbye to Clarry and his family I walked across town to the place where I was told the men were going to gather. I was shown photographs of some of their projects and listened to the story of the bushfire that had been skirting the town for the past few days. I'd thought it was just a series of fuel-reduction burns before the wet season.

I was unprepared for the meeting to be convened by Pastor David, who segued from the story of the bushfire to the AFL grand final to terrorism in about three sentences. He then announced that the subject for the evening was to be 'fear'.

I realised I was witnessing part of the long lineage of white missionary work in the community. I felt more uneasy as he went on to talk of the possibility of terrorist attacks in Australia and, remarkably, even in Hope Vale. He spoke of public beheadings, of trucks carrying fertiliser that could be used for making bombs and about placing our faith in Jesus to protect us from all of this evil. Fairly soon it became clear that fear wasn't the subject but the intention of the meeting. I burst in, unable to contain myself.

'But we have to remember that since 1914, since the British went to war with the Germans, because the Germans were building the Berlin to Baghdad Railway that would supply Mesopotamian, now Iraqi, oil to the German navy, that it's been 100 years of western countries dropping bombs on Arab states so that we can all drive, fly and boat about.'

I couldn't stop. 'Hope Vale is not a target. Sydney and Melbourne are, and Canberra, because that's where it's decided who gets bombed and who doesn't.'

I glanced at David, surprised to see he wasn't hostile. 'You can't produce peace by bombing people. Australia is also responsible for the escalation in violence.'

Hope Vale

The discussion, thankfully, was taken up by one of the older men who brought up that Abraham was a prophet of Jews, Christians and Muslims. He was evidently trying to find a place of accord in the room.

On the way home I apologised to Tim for interrupting the meeting. Tim nodded as he drove through the dark scrub, squinting. His silence gave me time to consider my actions. Tim was a friend of David's, at the very least a community friend. I was nothing but an interloper; at best, a guest. It wasn't my business to question Tim's signing of the mining agreement either. I just couldn't see how it wasn't a form of economic assimilation. But I recognised how these big political thoughts pushed me away from him, but in making the brews together I was brought close to Clarry.

When we got back home Meg and Elaine had prepared a feast to celebrate a last meal together. After the meal I set up my camera outside on the verandah for a group shot. Looking at the image now, I could easily have passed as a missionary: I was more neatly dressed than usual, my moustache looked extra creepy, and there is something distant about my eyes. Perhaps this is what happens to white guys who try to do 'good' in an Aboriginal community – they become something other than what they set out to be because their externalities cause division. Perhaps I was seeing in myself what I disliked about other men. Men such as Pastor David.

In a way, I *was* a preacher. Not one selling hope

or a god or the chance for greater affluence, but trying to peddle the very old idea of an almost lost sense of freedom – the taste and the hunt of it, the hardship and the love of it. I wondered if my unsettledness was more than feeling terrible about interjecting; perhaps it was my newcomer spirit mixing roughly with the old Guugu Yimithirr spirits. Perhaps it was something bigger, or littler. Perhaps it was time to turn for home.

Heading home

– Meg –

HOPEVALE *to* DAYLESFORD
4500 KILOMETRES
15 October 2014 to 8 January 2015

Leaving Tim and Elaine's and their community meant that we were finally turning south after ten-and-a-half months. We were only several kilometres out from Hope Vale when things started to feel very strange. We were going home.

We had about 400 kilometres to ride along the Mulligan Highway before we reunited with Zeph in Cairns. He was sending himself off to a conservative, all-boys Catholic school in Ballarat next year, one he had been determined to get into. We were really looking forward to having these last three months with him before we lost him to the world of high school.

The inland trip back was hot, exhausting and depressing. Dry, cattle-destroyed soils and rivers. Long endless roads of bitumen and roadkill. One billion termite mounds. We nearly ran out of water for the second time and hobbled into Cairns with a few days to rest before the Indigenous men's health conference and Zeph's arrival.

'Where's the nearest chicken coop?' Zephyr had barely hugged us all hello before he was pulling me over to the wall beside a line of luggage trolleys, making me stand beside him.

'Ooh nearly!' Patrick said, his hands on top of our heads. 'About this much to go.' He held up his thumb and pointer to show about a centimetre.

Years earlier, I had told Zeph that as soon as he was taller than me, as penance, he would have to sleep outside in our chicken coop.

'Come here, shorty,' I said to our lanky twelve-year-old, pulling him into a big squeezy cuddle.

Outside the airport, after greeting Zero, Zephyr put on his helmet like no time had been lost, and everything felt in its proper place again.

'Hello Zeph!' Woody called out repeatedly, all the way back to our magic caravan. 'Hello Zeph! Hello Zeph!'

'Hello Wooooooooodeeeeeee!' his big brother sang back.

We had met Sarah and Renee via Warm Showers, and they had kindly set up their backyard caravan for us. While I made lunch and Patrick made up Zeph's bed,

Heading home

Zeph and Woody rumbled on the grass outside.

'I can't believe it,' Zeph kept saying as we sat under the big mango tree to eat sandwiches. 'You're such a big boy now, Woody. When I left you were just a smiley little blob.'

For the three days Patrick was at the conference, Zephyr, Woody, Zero and I explored Cairns: swimming every day in the esplanade lagoon, fishing off the marina pier, getting to know our hosts and continuing our plant research. The first new species we found was a tamarind tree, which Woody and I especially loved, squeezing from the brown pods the sour, sticky fruit.

As Patrick rode the tandem to the conference each day, Zeph borrowed Renee's BMX.

'Can I please get my own bike?' Zeph pleaded. We were riding side by side after breakfast to the lagoon for a morning swim.

'You have your own bike at home,' I reminded him. 'In fact you've got two; one at our place and one at your mum's.'

'When we leave Cairns, I mean. Please! I really want my own bike.'

When I was about Zeph's age, I rode with my father on the back of a tandem. I had loved it. We talked for hours and I practised my timestables and sang a song my dad made up to help me learn fractions.

But Zeph was a different kind of kid, wanting his own adventure. We were ready for the next adventure too. For eleven months we had adjusted to the daily changes and rhythms of travelling the country by bike.

But all that was about to change.

In the five or so years our family had been car-free we had hired a car once and borrowed friends' cars a handful of times. We knew back at Hervey Bay that if we were going to cycle for fourteen months we would've had to turn south then, and miss out on travelling to far north Queensland. We explored various alternatives, but travelling with a dog and two kids made train travel fairly impossible. We went to a truck refuelling station and asked a couple of drivers what the likelihood was of hitching a ride but they both said the same thing: they weren't allowed to because of public liability.

The only option we had left was to hire a car so we could drive to Sydney, and send our bikes by truck. Both before and during the trip we had been fiercely saving money so we could continue travelling. Spending it on car hire and petrol wasn't what we had planned, but it had let us travel as far north as Hope Vale.

Up until that most northern point we had cycled around 6000 kilometres, although this didn't include the incidental everyday kilometres we clocked up riding around the places we camped at, getting supplies, making small transits out to the fishing spots locals told us about.

Then, as soon as Patrick's conference finished, we were zooming, shut off from the dirt and dust, the wind and trees, the birds and insects and all the dead things of the road we had sided with. It made us sick. Literally. Twenty minutes after we kissed Sarah, Renee and their boy Oscar goodbye, Woody vomited up his porridge and I couldn't stop crying. We cleaned Woody up and we all got out of the car.

'It's going to be OK,' Patrick said to me softly, as I sat on the ground feeding Woody. I heard him but it made no difference. He crouched beside me and rubbed my back.

'This is the worst!' I howled. 'I feel like we're undoing all our work. I feel like such a hypocrite.'

'I know, me too,' he said.

'Not me!' said Zeph. 'This is the best day ever! Cars are the best!'

'You're right, they are the best,' Patrick said.

Zeph's questions – 'What's wrong with McDonald's?', 'If flying was so bad, wouldn't the government make it illegal?' – provoked us. We knew he was just pushing our hippy buttons and that we were taking ourselves too seriously. But at the same time we also knew he was representing a cultural leviathan, one that hurls billions of dollars of clever propaganda at children and adults.

We got back in the car and turned the aircon on high.

Aircon!

Zeph read his book while Patrick drove. Woody and I tried to sing some of our songs, but in the void of the speeding car, they had no agency. I went back to feeling sick and sorry for myself. Then, after 165 kilometres that would have taken us three or more days to ride, we arrived at a free campsite in Mount Garnet.

Patrick set up our tents on the brown dry grass, Zeph

dug a fire pit and Woody and I collected fallen wood from around the giant termite mounds that dotted the reserve. As soon as Zeph struck the match, everything shifted, and all at once we were able to reclaim some of what we had lost.

'Mlwooouugh!' Zeph said, clutching his stomach.

'Mlwuuuuuuu!' I said, clutching mine.

One by one we all took turns reenacting Woody vomiting in the car, our feelings of uneasiness replaced with uproariousness. We cooked a simple pasta dish on the fire and sat on the dirt to eat.

The heart of the Queensland dustlands – cattle and coal – was quite a contrast to the coast's lush sugarcane fields and reef tourism. Zeph read books, one after another, while the rest of us stared goggled-eyed and mute out the windows. There would have been little chance of us cycling this route with such large distances between towns and so few opportunities to refill water bottles.

The breaks from being in the car were celebrated, but also made no sense. On our bikes we arrived in our own time. We huffed and puffed, sweated and sang and felt the winds change. Now when we arrived somewhere we had no relationship to the journey. When we met people I didn't feel like sharing our story. I felt like a fraud. And when we did share, I certainly didn't enjoy their enthusiasm.

'You must be so happy to be having a break,' a number of people said.

Heading home

I didn't feel this way at all.

For eleven months we had grown immune to the weather: riding in it, eating in it, sleeping in it. For the first time in nearly a year we all had sore throats and flu-like symptoms.

Just south of the NSW border we hurtled to visit Gary Trindall in Walgett. Gary, a Gamilaraay man Patrick met at the Cairns conference, welcomed us. While Zeph played with his two grandsons, Gary shared with us a few of his bush medicines, made from black wilga and boobialla trees, the leaves of which he made into brews to treat numerous ailments from arthritis to cancer.

At the conference, Gary had presented a paper with his NSW/ACT Aboriginal Legal Service colleagues about the Custody Notification Service, a program that has ensured that no Aboriginal deaths in custody have occurred since it was introduced. Gary's was just one of the papers that left an impression on Patrick, and one of several men Patrick would remain in contact with.

As we dropped further south into NSW the land changed: the climate cooled, the paddocks were more lush and dotted with dams. It had been many months since we'd witnessed cool-climate weeds such as plantain, dock and clover. It reminded us of the weed salads we made back home, using twenty or so species drizzled with olive oil and homemade vinegar. I wanted to keep riding our bikes forever, but at the same time, this land evoked in me steady pangs of solastalgia, and a deep longing for home.

And then, as if by magic, as though we had been inside a hypnotic bubble for the last ten days, it was over. We pulled into the driveway of Patrick's sister's family home in northern Sydney, and we all exhaled loudly. We erupted from the car after having travelled 2800 kilometres using 170 litres of unleaded petrol with a fuel cost of $250, happy to see our family and our bikes. We had dusted them off before loading them onto a truck in Cairns, but in the spotless Sydney suburb, they looked filthy, still covered in Hope Vale dirt.

We lived a very different life from Henny, Ant and their girls, but it was always so good to see them, and for the cousins to get reacquainted, spend hours on the trampoline, share meals and movies and games, pore through the latest magazines, and go for long walks down to the harbour.

On the day we were to leave Sydney, Patrick read out a letter to the editor in the *Sydney Morning Herald*, while I made us tea and toast.

'"More than 90 per cent of Australia's fuel is imported,"' he read. '"More than half of our petrol and diesel comes from a single refinery in Singapore. If that single point of supply fails, then within 12 days we are out of fuel. No planes, no cars, no trucks, no transport. In fact, a huge reduction in electricity."

'Imagine – no economy and no agriculture. My edible weed walks would be popular!' he laughed.

'Woo hoo!' I sang out. 'Bring it on!'

'"Coal-powered power stations will grind to a halt as it is diesel that keeps the coal moving to the turbines,"' he continued. '"The only power left will be hydro, wind and solar. What are the government plans for an Australia without oil-based fuels?"'

The house was abuzz with screaming kids gone crazy by the prospect of our looming departure. All our panniers were in various states of being packed, the kitchen was in disarray with breakfast dishes, and Zero and Henny's dog Friday were chasing each other around the house. But when Patrick closed the paper and we looked at each other, the house momentarily went quiet. The letter confirmed what we'd been saying all along. It was just what we needed to be reminded of on the day we were to resume our ride. In our hire car and in Sydney's affluent suburbs I had lost my enthusiasm. Now I felt my resolve return.

I felt galvanised. Yes, it had been lovely to catch up with family, but it was time to get back to work: to wave the flag of simplicity, of low-consumption living, to continue to prepare for less certain times, to be strong and brave and know up close our limits and our vulnerabilities.

After a noisy, rushed, school-morning kind of goodbye, we were off. We would have loved to have stayed until Christmas, but it was still seven weeks away.

Some relationships are fiery and passionate, defined by difference. Patrick's and mine is defined by our values. But like most couples, we agree on the big picture and sometimes get caught up in the small stuff. When we do, it's usually a minor explosion and then it's over. During our trip, we bickered because we were tired, usually at the end of a big day, but on our way to the Southern Highlands we had a doozie over our morning cuppa.

'Please don't give it all to Zeph,' I said. We'd stopped at the Bargo Pie Shop for a fairly ordinary and expensive refuelling.

Patrick looked up at me, continuing to pour the milk from his small jug into Zeph's glass.

'Can you give some to Woody?'

'He can have yours,' Patrick said.

On the occasions we went out for tea, that's how it went: Patrick, who didn't take his tea white, gave his milk to Zeph, and I poured for Woody whatever milk was left that I didn't use.

'I've drunk all mine,' I said, turning the small jug upside-down over my teacup to show it was empty.

While we played out this petty domestic scene, Zeph lifted his glass and quickly drained the contents.

'Great!' I shouted. 'You and Zeph get drinks and food. And Woody gets nothing.'

'Woody gets your boob,' Patrick snapped back, 'more bloody nourishment than any of this shit.'

Angry words were spat and hissed. Two other patrons, seated behind us, glanced over. The table was bumped and everything rattled. Woody started to cry.

'Let's go, Zeph,' Patrick rose. 'I can't stand this any longer.'

I quickly paid the bill, avoiding eye contact with the lady behind the counter, and carried Woody outside.

Heading home

'Where's Dada and Zephyr?' I asked him.

'Where's Zero?' he asked me back.

We stood outside the café for several minutes, waiting for the others to appear before it dawned on me that they had gone. It was a first.

I felt stunned and scared, but also relieved that I wouldn't have to face Patrick. I put Woody in his seat, tickling him and laughing to hide my fear that we'd been abandoned. I looked up the GPS to decide on a route to Moss Vale. Bike route or car? I was petrified I'd make the wrong decision.

I have a notoriously bad sense of direction. We climbed for almost two hours on our way to the highlands, the air becoming cooler as we ascended. You're doing it! I thought to myself.

'I can't believe how stubborn you are!' Patrick said to me once I'd caught up on Mount Gibraltar, just before our descent into Bowral.

'This is all about you seeing your parents, isn't it?' I shot back. 'You've been so on edge today.'

In previous years when we'd travelled to NSW to see Patrick's folks he'd often been just as agitated. I knew how he felt. On some occasions I'd also experienced the same thing with my family.

'I'm just tired and fed up and everything's too hard at the moment,' he called out.

'Come on guys!' Zeph said. 'Keep it together. You're supposed to be the adults!'

At Bradman Oval in Bowral, where Patrick grew up playing cricket and where we stopped to make lunch, we found salsify growing in the gardens, which we dug up to take as a gift for his parents, whom we were spending the night with. We cleaned and grated the parsnip-like roots and offered them raw, drizzled in lemon juice, to Nana and Papa.

The next day, we rode a short distance to Patrick's brother Sam and his family's house and set up our tents in their backyard, just near where Patrick and Zeph were to spend the next week building a chicken coop.

We were about to celebrate our one-year anniversary of being on the road. Once again I was reminded of what returning home might feel like. I loved how Patrick's folks lived so close to Sam's boys and how involved they were in their lives, and looked forward to Woody sharing that with my parents when we returned. I was also looking forward to Woody knowing our chooks and ducks, and the daily routine around them that provided us with fresh organic eggs. Every day!

At Plantation Point, 85 kilometres from Moss Vale, we set up camp above a cliff overlooking the rocks at Jervis Bay. For four quiet days we swam and fished, ate rock oysters, documented the seaweeds we found, and started talking seriously about how we felt about going home and how we wanted to live when we returned. Would we stay in our house or sell up? Could we really live, as we dreamed, with no electricity, not even solar?

Heading home

How would we reduce the risk of volunteer burnout again? Maybe we could extend our garden love-shack and invite another family to come and live with us, to help share the load of gardening, cooking and parenting. Maybe we would move in ourselves and rent out the main house. One thing we agreed on was that we wouldn't move back into the house right away. We would put our tents up in the garden and live there for as long as the weather permitted before making the transition indoors.

'That's a great idea!' Zeph added. 'Then I can have the house to myself.'

Only 8 kilometres away, we found a secluded campsite at Sanctuary Point. Just before bed, Woody and I went for a walk along the edge of St George's Basin. I opened my notebook as we slowly strolled. Lessons from the road to take back home, I wrote, then underlined. I looked over at Woody, who was gathering rocks, trying to skim them as Zeph had showed him. I began my list:

1. Live outside as much as possible.
2. Avoid chairs.
3. Campfires make home.

On our way back to camp I found some small red berries I didn't recognise. Despite our research, it was not uncommon for us to find things we'd never seen before. I plucked a few from the top of the bush to show

Patrick, then looked down to see Woody stuffing some of the fruits into his mouth.

'NO!' I yelled, grabbing his wrist.

He was normally so cautious, asking before he ate anything he found, but I guess he saw me picking the fruit and assumed they were OK. I flicked out the berries that were in his mouth but could see by the red pulp in his teeth that he had swallowed some already. Shit! What had I done? It was a parent's worst nightmare.

I scooped him up and ran back to Patrick and showed him the fruit in my hand. He couldn't identify it either. I got Woody ready for bed and fed him to sleep, quietly sobbing. Patrick and I had a mostly sleepless night. If it wasn't anxiety that kept us up, it was the rain that we worried would flood our camp.

And oh, how it rained. I was, as you can imagine, overjoyed when Woody woke calling for a feed at 6 am. We packed up our saturated tents between showers, scrunching our wet gear into our panniers. It would be a while yet before the headlines would stop flashing through my mind: TODDLER DIES FROM EATING BERRIES: FORAGING MOTHER TO BLAME.

For the first twelve months of our trip we could have counted the days we were rained on on one tanned hand. This stretch along the NSW south coast certainly made up for such a dry year on the road. Although we knew that this was what living outside was all about, we were getting tired of the extra work the rain brought.

Heading home

With the promise of another 20 to 40 mm, we packed up our tents at Mystery Bay, and pedalled the 30 kilometres to Cobargo to stay with a kindred spirit we'd met online.

Even though Ronnie had warned us that the stretch of road just north of her place was extremely dangerous, we brushed it off – all roads in Australia are dangerous for bike-riders, we scoffed – and took the road, declining her kind offer to pick us up in her ute. But despite how cautiously we rode, and despite our flag and lights and bright clothing and rear-view helmet mirrors and defensive riding, some drivers just don't think cyclists are entitled to be on the road. It was on this stretch that we had our closest call by far.

The tandem's gears were playing up so at the bottom of a particularly steep hill, Zephyr hopped off the bike so Patrick could adjust the gears manually. I overtook them and headed on up the hill with Woody, my cheer-squad captain, urging me on with the uphill song. As Ronnie had warned, there were no shoulders, just a thin uneven path of dirt and fallen sticks between the bitumen and the edge of the cutting.

In my mirror I could see a large truck coming up behind me. This was no big deal; over the last year I had seen thousands of trucks. The truck raced up the hill, not taking my presence or the road conditions into account. Or the truck that he didn't know was coming the other way, that was hurtling over the crest. When I sensed the truck behind me wasn't going to slow down, I got the hell off the road and squished as far over to the left as I could get, ending up in the drain. By this point in our trip we were certainly hardy to all kinds of vehicles and events that had frightened the hell out of us when we first left home.

But this time was different.

I usually rode at the back of our small convoy, from where I had witnessed many cars zooming past too close to the tandem and had felt my heart skip a beat too many times. So I hoped Patrick was still tinkering with his gears, and hadn't seen how close the truck had come to my bike. I knew it would upset him. But see it he did.

We pulled over at the first safe opportunity we found, a few hills later, into somebody's driveway. I got Woody down from the bike so I could properly rest and breathe and recover and go over with Zeph and Patrick what had happened. While we hugged and talked and felt ridiculously lucky, a highway patrol car pulled up. The policeman told us he'd just spoken to the truck driver who'd called us irresponsible for riding these roads and how he'd nearly hit me because I had been riding in the middle of the lane.

'Riding in the middle of the lane?' I yelled. 'I'm sorry, but if I had been in the middle of the lane I would be dead, because he was driving like a maniac. What a liar!'

Patrick took over from there, explaining how the truck had passed me recklessly, over double white lines on the crest of a hill.

'We have every right to be on these roads,' Patrick concluded.

We waited for the officer to agree, but he wasn't

forthcoming. Even when we weren't breaking the law we felt like illegitimates.

From the logo on the side of the truck, Patrick was able to look up the company and call the head office to report the case. The next day at Ronnie's house, the manager called back to report that he had reviewed the footage taken on the truck's camera and could confirm my bike was as far off the bitumen as it could go, and not in the middle of the road as the driver had stated. We were relieved by his honesty, but he wasn't interested in Patrick's suggestion that his drivers take a bicycle awareness course. The manager couldn't work out what we were doing on that road with our kids.

Over the Victorian border in Cann River, Zero found and put out of its misery a brushtail possum that had been hit by a car. After setting up camp above the river, we lit a small fire and stewed the possum in the billy with garlic, carrots, tomato, salt, pepper and a handful of buckshorn plantain growing nearby, the seed heads of which are mucilaginous, which helped thicken the stew. Over the five or so hours of slow cooking, our campsite grew to include Doris the vintage bike and her rider Connor, a dancer from Leeds in the UK. Just after dinner we welcomed another cycle-tourist, Nathan from New Zealand, though unfortunately by then, the possum had been devoured alongside the damper Zeph had made.

In a reserve on the outskirts of Hurstbridge, only 50 kilometres from Melbourne, we camped for two nights.

'How's your list going?' Patrick asked, lying beside me in our tent.

'Good,' I said. 'Though I think I'm in denial.'

'In denial of what?'

'It doesn't feel quite real that we'll be back in Daylesford in a few days. I'm still not ready to go home. I still don't want to.'

'Maybe you just need a little nudging,' he offered. 'To leave in the first place, and then to come home. You are a stubborn Capricorn.'

'I think you're right,' I said. 'Every time I imagine us at home I picture being on my bike, with Woody in his seat, going around and around the roundabout at the bottom of the main street. What do people do at home?'

'They lead meaningful lives.'

'I know. But after all this time away, I just can't picture being at home and finding that.'

'You don't find it,' he said, propping himself up on his elbows, turning his head-torch to the side so as not to blind me. 'You create it. We create it. We're both in this together.'

He leant over and we kissed. 'Now, read me your list!'

'OK,' I said, finding the page again.

4. Electricity disrupts.
5. Time is not money.
6. Balance being quiet with being social.

Heading home

    7. Reduce online time.

    'Anything else?' Patrick thought for a while, then added:

    8. Possessions equal complications.
    9. Joy and pain are intertwined.
    10. Food is everywhere.

'I reckon I'm the only kid who has ever pedalled all this way up and down the country,' Zeph said as we set up our tents for the last time, just over a small footbridge in the bush near the Woodend Community Garden.
    'I reckon you're right,' Patrick said.
    'From the Southern Highlands to Coffs Harbour and then from Sydney to Daylesford. I'm so cool!'
    'We're not home yet,' Patrick teased. 'We've still got 45 kilometres to ride tomorrow.'
    That night in bed I read to Patrick the last items on my list.

    11. Be more generous than you have to be.
    12. Sharing stories and food makes life rich.

    I exhaled loudly, pleased with myself.
    'Hang on, there's one more, a baker's dozen,' Patrick said excitedly.

    13. Free is freeing.

I added it to the bottom of the page.

In the morning, as we packed up our wet tents for the last time, I felt giddy with excitement, with pride and foreboding. What was life at home going to be like? How were we going to make sure that these 400 days away didn't just become the memories we would hold dear and call upon, like a jukebox, as we aged and sank back into settled life?

We spent the following hours drifting in an excited, dreamy state. We were ready to go home but happy to delay our landing too.

And then all of a sudden, we were on our way and it was raining but we were too exhilarated to pull over and put on our rain jackets.

I couldn't stop crying. We were fluttering. Through the glorious arch of a rainbow at Tylden. We were flying. Past the steaming volcanic potato fields of Trentham. We were gliding. Down from the peaks of Bullarto, cutting through the dense woodland road of the Wombat State Forest. I felt so lightheaded I wasn't sure how I was managing to keep my heavy bike upright, but my legs had never felt so strong.

'Woo hoo!!' We all took turns yelling. 'Woo hooooooo!'

'That's where the Sunday market is!' I called out to Woody.

Now that we were home I was looking forward, more than anything, to showing him around his town.

Heading home

'There's Rea Lands Park Community Garden! This is your home!' I cried. 'This is our home!'

I didn't know it at the time, but Patrick had also cried the whole way through the forest from Bullarto. Where mine were intense tears of triumph and joy mixed with the thud of arrival, his had been tears of relief. We had made it home without any of us being injured or killed, a weight he had been bearing.

We were met at the Albert Street Community Garden by family and friends who cheered and whooped and yelled as we rode into view. As we approached the garden, where I had fallen fourteen months earlier, Patrick, in the excitement of the moment, miscalculated a turn and tipped the tandem over, careening himself and his two passengers, unhurt, over the finish line. We had come full circle.

The celebration continued back at our empty house, where our dear friend Pete had strung his hand-painted banner, 'WE LOVE YOU, ARTIST AS FAMILY'. We excitedly caught up with our friends' news, new babies, new houses, new jobs, and the garden. Baby chicks! Peaches! Plums! Apples! Pears! Kiwifruit! Grapes!

And when the last of the welcome-home revellers left, we were once again alone, in our quiet house. The rain continued to fall, but we were dry. The wind continued to lash, but we couldn't feel it, just a strange new feeling of a familiarity that was unfamiliar.

Although we had been determined to set up our tents and sleep in the garden for as long as we needed, the rain had other plans. We carried our mattresses from where they'd been stored in the SWAP shed and set them up under our sleeping bags. We were exhausted from the ride and from the emotion, but we still had one more thing to do.

We trudged over in the mud back to the shed and carried our wooden kitchen table over to the house. We had been talking about doing this for months and it felt like a good first thing to do, to bring into our home what we loved so much about camp life and living on the ground.

Patrick found the handsaw in one of the bikeport tool cupboards and held it up in front of the table legs. He and Zephyr had made the table for me and had given it to me for my birthday a few months after we first got together.

'Are you sure you're ready for this?' he asked, his mouth an enormous smile, his eyes bright and excited.

'I'm in,' I whispered.

What we took when we left home

MEG
Kona Ute cargo bike, with Woody in a rear-mounted child seat
Total weight including bodies, gear and bike = 128.5 kg

Handlebar bag: Emergency toilet paper (small roll), riding gloves, tin whistle, sunglasses, notebook, earplugs, sunscreen, small tupperware (Zero water bowl), 2 x sun visors (to wear under helmets on sunny days), hanky, lipbalm, high-visibility vest, head torch, sports whistle, 750 ml water bottle, padlock, keys, phone charger, handbag (incl. pocketknife, phone), waterproof protector for handlebar bag, wallet.

Pannier 1, red rear left: Woody's clothes bag #1 (bottoms) including winter and summer sleeping bags.

Pannier 2, red rear right: Woody's clothes bag #2 (tops) including inflatable sleeping mat and towel.

Rack pack 1, yellow rear: Woody's compostable nappies, wipes, sunscreen, toilet paper, small tupperware.

Pannier 3, blue front left: Zeph's clothes, sunglasses, towel, sleeping bag, sleeping mat, hiking pillow, goggles and snorkel, riding gloves, fish catch bag, 2 bike cables.

Pannier 4, blue front right: Meg's clothes, book, toiletry bag, tampons.

Storage under Woody's seat: 1 fold-down hand spear (fish), 1 fold-down longbow, 3 arrows.

Water: 2 x 750 ml stainless-steel water bottles (3 bottles in total).

PATRICK AND ZEPHYR
Holstar Grand Tourer tandem bike, with Zero in front basket
Total weight including bodies, gear and bike = 175.2 kg

Handlebar bag: Camera, 2 x memory cards, camera lead and charger, permanent marker, memory stick, fluoro ankle straps, high-visibility vest, sunscreen, Zero's lead, 2 x padlock, keys, riding gloves, head torch, sunglasses, waterproof protector for handlebar bag, phone and charger, maps, hunting knife, knife pouch, knife sharpener, wallet.

What we took when we left home

Pannier 5, yellow rear left: Food bag (3 kg organic oats, 3 kg organic spelt pasta, large bag of AaF sun-dried apples and plums, large bag of AaF sun-cured lemongrass, AaF sun-dried cayenne peppers, 30 heads AaF garlic, small chopping board).

Pannier 6, yellow rear right: PJ clothes, book and laptop.

Rack pack 2, yellow rear: Laundry bag, universal laundry plug, laundry soap bar and container, ergo baby carrier, folding bucket (10 L), clothesline and pegs, foraging bag, root tool, small hatchet, small handsaw, 4 x rain jackets, calico shopping bag, 2 x spare stuff sacks, 2 x bike chargers and leads, double adapter, 2 x spare tubes, PJ field notes and drawing equipment, first-aid kit, solar monkey.

Pannier 7, yellow front left: Kitchen bag (10 L folding bucket, 3 pot kit, pot holder, 4 x sporks, 3 x small cups, 2 fuel stove cans, 1 x kitchen knife, 3 x box of matches, 1 x hiking gas burner, 1 x tea towel, 1 x pot scourer/ sponge.

Pannier 8, yellow front right: Meg and PJ bedding (2 x sleeping bags, 2 x sleeping mats, 2 x hiking pillows, 2 x cotton liners).

Tool bag (under seat): Chain lube, self-adhesive water proof patches, small screwdriver, 1 x large allen key,

4 x spare disc break pads (Meg), 2 x spare disc break pads (PJ), allen key set, spare tube valves, spare chain links, chain breaker, spare allen bolts, spoke key, electrical tape, 2 x tube repair kits, shifting spanner, 3 x tyre levers, packet of cable ties, small cable snips, oil rag, 2 x bike charger fuses.

Rear rack: 2 x 2-person hiking tents, 1 x tarpaulin.

Water: 5 stainless-steel water bottles (various sizes).

Our list of free food and medicine

(Naturalised, indigenous, newcomer, weedy, autonomous, feral – 256 species and counting)

Warning: wrongly identified or prepared could prove fatal. Consult experts and knowledge holders before use. A small number of species listed may be protected, rare and/or endangered and are listed here only for survival purposes.

African tulip tree (*Spathodea campanulata nilotica*)
Amaranths (*Amaranthus* spp.)
Asthma plant (*Chamaesyce hirta*)
Australian barracuda (*Sphyraena novaehollandiae*)
Australian bugle (*Ajuga australis*)
Australian herring (*Arripis georgianus*)
Australian honey fungus (*Armillaria luteobubalina*)
Australian long-finned eel (*Anguilla reinhardtii*)
Australian short-finned eel (*Anguilla australis*)
Australian wood duck (*Chenonetta jubata*)
Bamboo (*Bambusa* spp.)
Banana (*Musa* spp.)

Banana passionfruit (*Passiflora tarminiana*)
Barracuda (*Sphyraena* spp.)
Barred queenfish (*Scomberoides tala*)
Beach cherry (*Eugenia reinwardtiana*)
Beefsteak fungus (*Fistulina hepatica*)
Bittercress (*Cardamine hirsuta*)
Blackberry (*Rubus ursinus*)
Black bream (*Hephaestus fuliginosus*)
Black nightshade (*Solanum nigrim*)
Black wilga (*Geijera parviflora*)
Blowfly grass (*Briza maxima*)
Bloodwood apple (*Cystococcus* spp.)
Blue quandong (*Elaeocarpus grandis*)
Blue swimmer crab (*Portunus pelagicus*)
Blue-staining meanie (*Psilocybe subaeruginosa*)
Boab tree (*Adansonia gregorii*)
Boneseed (*Chrysanthemoides monilifera*)
Boobialla (*Myoporum insulare*)
Bower spinach (*Tetragonia implexicoma*)
Boxthorns (*Lycium* spp.)
Bracken (*Pteridium esculentum*)
Brazilian cherry (*Eugenia uniflora*)
Broad-leaf native cherry (*Exocarpos latifolius*)
Broom (*Cytisus scoparius*)
Brown trout (*Salmo trutta*)
Brushtail possum (*Trichosurus*)
Buckshorn plantain (*Plantago coronopus*)
Bulrush (*Typha*)
Burdekin plum (*Pleiogynium timorense*)
Burdock (*Arctium*)

Our list of free food and medicine

Bursaria (*Bursaria spinosa*)
Bush lemon (*Citrus limon*)
Bush banana (*Marsdenia australis*)
Bush passionfruit (*Passiflora foetida*)
Cabbage tree palm (*Livistona* spp.)
Cairns fan palm (*Licuala ramsayi*)
Candlenut (*Aleurites moluccana*)
Cape gooseberry (*Physalis peruvians*)
Cardoon (*Cynara cardunculus*)
Carp (*Cyprinus carpio*)
Chanterelle (*Cantharellus*)
Cherry plum (*Prunus cerasifera*)
Cherry ballart (*Exocarpos cupressiformis*)
Chickweed (*Stellaria media*)
Chinee apple (*Ziziphus mauritiana*)
Chiton (*Chiton* spp.)
Cleavers (*Galium*)
Clover (*Trifolium*)
Cluster fig (*Ficus racemosa*)
Cobbler's pegs (*Bidens pilosa*)
Cocky apple (*Planchonia careya*)
Coconut palm (*Cocos nucifera*)
Common brushtail possum (*Trichosurus vulpecula*)
Cotton tree (*Hibiscus tiliaceus*)
Cranesbills (*Geranium* spp.)
Custard apple (*Annona squamosa*)
Dandelion (*Taraxacum*)
Davidson's plum (*Davidsonia pruriens*)
Daylily (*Hemerocallis fulva*)
Deadnettle (*Lamium*)

Devil's fig (*Solanum torvum*)
Devil's guts (*Cassytha* spp.)
Docks (*Rumex* spp.)
Dusky flathead (*Platycephalus fuscus*)
Eastern grey kangaroo (*Macropus giganteus*)
Elderberry (*Sambucus*)
Emu berry (*Grewia retusifloia*)
European honey bee (*Apis mellifera*)
European rabbit (*Oryctolagus cuniculus*)
Fathen (*Chenopodium album*)
Fennel (*Foeniculum*)
Feral deer (*Dama dama; Rusa timorensis; Axis axis*)
Feral goat (*Capra hircus*)
Feral pig (*Sus scrofa*)
Field mushroom (*Agaricus campestris*)
Fig (*Ficus carica*)
Flatweed (*Hypochoeris*)
Flax lily (*Dianella* spp.)
Fleabane (*Conyza* spp.)
Freshwater crayfish (*Euastacus armatus*)
Freshwater mussel (*Velesunio* spp.)
Fumitory (*Fumaria*)
Garden snail (*Helix aspersa*)
Geebung (*Persoonia falcata*)
Gold cap mushroom (*Psilocybe subaeruginosa*)
Golden grevillea (*Grevillea pteridifolia*)
Golden trevally (*Gnathanodon speciosus*)
Gorse (*Ulex europaeus*)
Gotu kola (*Centella asiatica*)
Grass tree (*Xanthorrhoea* spp.)

Our list of free food and medicine

Great morinda (*Morinda citrifolia*)
Green tree ant (*Oecophylla smaragdina*)
Grey morwong (*Nemadactylus douglasii*)
Groundsel (*Senecio vulgaris*)
Guava (*Psidium guajava*)
Harrisia cactus (*Harrisia martini*)
Hawksbeard (*Crepis*)
Hawthorn (*Crataegus*)
Hedgehog fungus (*Hydnum repandum*)
Horehound (*Marrubium vulgar*)
Horse mushroom (*Agaricus arvensis*)
Inky cap (*Coprinopsis atramentaria*)
Jewfish (*Argyrosomus japonicus*)
Jerusalem thorn (*Parkinsonia aculeata*)
Kangaroo apple (*Solanum laciniatum*)
Knotweed (*Polygonum*)
Lady apple (*Syzguim suborbiculare*)
Lavender (*Lavandula* spp.)
Lawyer's wig (*Coprinus comatus*)
Leichardt tree (*Nauclea orientalis*)
Lemon balm (*Melissa officinalis*)
Lilly pilly (*Syzygium*)
Loquat (*Eriobotrya japonica*)
Macadamia (*Macadamia integrifolia*)
Marigold (*Calendula*)
Mat-rush (*Lomandra*)
Mallow (*Malva*)
Magpie goose (*Anseranas semipalmata*)
Mango (*Mangifera indica*)
Mangrove snail (*Nerita* spp.)

Milkmaids (*Burchardia umbellate*)
Milk thistle (*Silybum*)
Mistletoes (*Loranthaceae; Viscaceae*)
Mock orange (*Murraya paniculata*)
Mudcrab (*Scylla serrata*)
Mud mussel (*Polymesoda coaxans*)
Mud whelk (*Terebralia* spp.)
Murnong yam (*Microseris lanceolata*)
Murray spiny freshwater crayfish (*Euastacus armatus*)
Nardoo (*Marsilea drummondii*)
Nasturtium (*Tropaeolum majus*)
Native ginger (*Alpinia caerulea*)
Native gooseberry (*Physalis minima*)
Native kapok bush (*Cochlospermum fraseri*)
Native monstera (*Rhaphidophora pinnata*)
Native mulberry (*Hedycarya angustifolia*)
Native rock fig (*Ficus platypoda*)
Native rosella (*Hibiscus sabdariffa*)
Nectarine (*Prunus persica nectarina*)
Neem tree (*Azadirachta indica*)
Neptune's necklace (*Hormosira banksii*)
New Zealand spinach (*Tetragonia tetragonioides*)
Nonda plum (*Parinari nonda*)
Oaks (*Quercus* spp.)
Old man weed (*Centipeda cunninghamii*)
Queensland fruit-fly maggot (*Bactrocera tryoni*)
Oyster mushrooms (*Pleurotus ostreatus*)
Pacific rosewood (*Thespesia populneoides*)
Pandanus (*Pandanus* spp.)
Paperbark tree (*Melaleuca leucadendra*)

Our list of free food and medicine

Parasol mushroom (*Macrolepiota clelandii*)
Paterson's curse (*Echium plantagineum*)
Paw paw (*Carica papaya*)
Peach (*Prunus persica*)
Peanut tree (*Sterculia quadrifida*)
Petty spurge (*Euphorbia peplus*)
Phalsa (*Grewia asiatica*)
Pigface (*Carpobrotus* spp.)
Pipi (*Plebidonax deltoides*)
Plantain (*Plantago* spp.)
Pond apple (*Annona glabra*)
Poppy (*Papaver* spp.)
Prickly pear (*Opuntia stricta*)
Purslane (*Portulaca oleracea*)
Quandong (*Santalum lanceolatum*)
Ragwort (*Senico jacobaea*)
Rainbow trout (*Oncorhynchus mykiss*)
Redfin perch (*Perca fluviatilis*)
Rhubarb bolete (*Boletellus obscurecoccineus*)
Rock wallaby (*Petrogale*)
Ruby saltbush (*Enchylaena tomentosa*)
Saffron milkcap (*Lactarius deliciosus*)
Salsify (*Tragopogon*)
Scarlett pimpernel (*Anagallis arvensis*)
Scrub turpentine (*Canarium australianum*)
Scurvy weed (*Commelina* spp.)
Seaberry saltbush (*Rhagodia candolleana*)
Shaggy parasol (*Chlorophyllum brunneum*)
She-oak (*Casuarina equisetifolia*)
Shepherd's purse (*Capsella bursa-pastoris*)

Silk cotton tree (*Bombax ceiba*)
Slippery jack (*Suillus luteus*)
Sheep sorrel (*Rumex acetosella*)
Snakeweed (*Stachytarpheta indica*)
Soap tree (*Alphitonia excelsa*)
Soursob (*Oxalis pes-caprae*)
Southern garfish (*Hyporhamphus melanochir*)
Southern mud oyster (*Ostrea angasi*)
Southern yellowtail (*Seriola lalandi lalandi*)
Sow thistle (*Sonchus* spp.)
Spanish mackerel (*Scomberomorus commerson*)
Spearmint (*Mentha spicata*)
Spear thistle (*Cirsium vulgare*)
Star apple (*Chrysophyllum cainito*)
Stinging nettle (*Urtica dioica*)
St John's wort (*Hypericum perforatum*)
Storksbill (*Erodium cicutarium*)
Swallow-tailed dart (*Trachinotus coppingeri*)
Swamp wallaby (*Wallabia bicolor*)
Sydney rock oyster (*Saccostrea glomerata*)
Tamarind (*Tamarindus indica*)
Taro (*Colocasia esculenta*)
The prince (*Agaricus augustus*)
Tree fern (*Cyathea* spp.)
Tropical almond (*Terminalia catappa*)
Vanilla lilies (*Arthropodium* spp.)
Variegated limpet (*Cellana tramoserica*)
Vetch (*Vicia*)
Vietnamese mint (*Persicaria odorata*)
Violet (*Viola* spp.)

Our list of free food and medicine

Walnut (*Juglans* sp.)
Watercress (*Nasturtium officinale*)
Waterlily (*Nymphaea* spp.)
Water ribbons (*Triglochin* spp.)
Wild apples (*Malus* spp.)
Wild cucumber (*Cucumis*)
Wild lettuce (*Lacula*)
Wild garlic (*Allium triquetrum*)
Wild mustard (*Brassica* sp.)
Wild radish (*Raphanus raphanistrum*)
Wild rocket (*Diplotaxis tenuifolia*)
Wild roses (*Rosaceae*)
Wild turnip (*Brassica* sp.)
Willow (*Salix* spp.)
Wood blewit (*Lepista nuda*)
Wood sorrel (*Oxalis*)
Yabby (*Cherax* spp.)
Yarrow (*Achillea millefolium*)
Yellow-eye mullet (*Aldrichetta forsteri*)
Yellowfin bream (*Acanthopagrus australis*)

Related reading

(Books that inspired and informed us)

David Abram, *Becoming Animal: An Earthly Cosmology*, New York: Pantheon Books, 2010.
Samuel Alexander, *Voluntary Simplicity: The poetic alternative to consumer culture*, New Zealand: Stead & Daughters Ltd., 2009.
John Berger, *Pig Earth*, London: Chatto & Windus, 1985.
Robyn Davidson, *Tracks: A Woman's Solo Trek across 1700 Miles of Australian Outback*, London: Jonathan Cape, 1980.
Tony Dingle, *Aboriginal Economy: Patterns of Experience*, Melbourne: McPhee Gribble/Penguin Books, 1988.
Claire Dunn, *My Year Without Matches: Escaping the City in Search of the Wild*, Melbourne: Black Inc., 2014.
W. Evans, *Diary of a Welsh Swagman*, Melbourne: Sun Books, 1975.
David Flemming, *Lean Logic: A Dictionary for the Future and How to Survive It*, England: The Estate of David Flemming, 2011.
Jonathan Safran Foer, *Eating Animals*, London: Hamish Hamilton, 2009.
Lionel Fogarty, *Minyung Woolah Binnung: What Saying Says*, Southport: Keeaira Press, 2004.
Greg Foyster, *Changing Gears: A Pedal-Powered Detour from the Rat Race*, Melbourne: Affirm Press, 2013.
Bruce Fuhrer, *A Field Companion to Australian Fungi*, South Yarra: Field Naturalists Club of Victoria, 1985.
Bill Gammage, *The Biggest Estate on Earth: How Aborigines Made Australia*, Crows Nest: Allen & Unwin, 2011.
Alan Garner, *Strandloper*, London: Harvill Press, 1996.
David Graeber, *Debt: The First 5000 Years*, Brooklyn: Melville House, 2011.
John Michael Greer, *The Long Descent: A User's Guide to the End of the*

Related reading

Industrial Age, Gabriola Island: New Society Publishers, 2008.

Adam Grubb & Annie Raser-Rowland, *The Weed Forager's Handbook: A Guide to Edible and Medicinal Weeds in Australia*, Melbourne: Hyland House, 2012.

Gunditjmara People with Wettenhall, Gib. *The People of Budj Bim*, Heywood, Victoria: em Press Publishing, 2010.

Shannon Hayes, *Radical Homemakers: Reclaiming Domesticity from a Consumer Culture*, Richmondville: Left to Write Press, 2010.

Les Hiddens, *Bush Tucker Field Guide*, Australia: Penguin Books, 2001.

Tom Hodgkinson, *The Idle Parent: Why Less Means More When Raising Kids*, USA: Penguin Books, 2009.

David Holmgren, *Future Scenarios: How Communities can Adapt to Peak Oil and Climate Change*, Vermont: Chelsea Green Publishers, 2009.

Chloe Hooper, *The Tall Man: Death and Life on Palm Island*, Australia: Penguin Books, 2008.

Derrick Jensen, *Listening to the Land: Conversations about Nature, Culture, and Eros*, Vermont: Chelsea Green Publishing Company, 2004.

Sandor Ellix Katz, *Wild Fermentation: The Flavour, Nutrition and Craft of Live-Culture Foods*, Vermont: Chelsea Green Publishing Company, 2003.

Tim Low, *Wild Food Plants of Australia*, Sydney: Angus & Robertson, 1988.

Rod Moss, *The Hard Light of Day: An Artist's Story of Friendships in Arrernte Country*, St Lucia: University of Queensland Press, 2010.

Stephen Muecke, *Ancient and Modern: Time, Culture, and Indigenous Philosophy*, Sydney: UNSW Press, 2004.

Anitra Nelson & Frans Timmerman. *Life Without Money: Building Fair and Sustainable Economies*, London: Pluto Press, 2011.

Oodgeroo, *My people*, Milton: John Wiley & Sons, (4th ed.) 2008.

Val Plumwood, *Environmental Culture: The Ecological Crisis of Reason*, London: Routledge, 2002.

Michael Pollan, *Cooked: A Natural History of Transformation*, London: Penguin Books, 2013.

C.M. Porter, G.C. Wescott & G.P. Quinn, *Life on the Rocky Shores of South-eastern Australia*, Melbourne: Victorian National Parks Association, 2010.

Padgett Powell, *The Interrogative Mood: A novel?*, London: Profile Books, 2009

Deborah Bird Rose, *Wild Dog Dreaming: Love and Extinction*, Charlottesville and London: University of Virginia Press, 2011.

Vandana Shiva, *Soil Not Oil: Environmental Justice in an Age of Climate Crisis*,

London: South End Press, 2008.
Rick Smith & Bruce Lourie, *Slow Death by Rubber Duck: The Secret Danger of Everyday Things*, Berkeley: Counterpoint, 2009.
Rebecca Solnit, *Wanderlust: A History of Walking*, New York: Penguin Books, 2001.
Paul Stamets, *Mycelium Running: How Mushrooms Can Help Save the World*, New York: Ten Speed Press, 2005.
Snu Vooglebreinder, *Garden of Eden: The Shamanic Use of Psychoactive Flora and Fauna, and the Study of Consciousness*, Victoria: self-published, 2009.
Maya Ward, *The Comfort of Water: A River Pilgrimage*, Yarraville: Transit Lounge Publishing, 2011.
McKenzie Wark, *A Hacker Manifesto*, Massachusetts: Harvard University Press, 2004.
Alexis Wright, *The Swan Book*, Sydney: Giramondo, 2014.
A.M. Young, *A Field Guide to the Fungi of Australia*, Sydney: University of New South Wales Press, 2005.
John Zerzan, *Running on Emptiness: The Pathology of Civilisation*, Los Angeles: Feral House, 2002.

We couldn't have done it without you

We thank the following for their love and support of our adventuring: Nicole Brammy, Joanne McCombe, April Phillips, Louise Doherty, Petra Bueskens, Nick Wong, Peter Brandis, Jason Maher, Juliette Anich, Tosh Szatow, Lee and Dave Edmonds, Sharonne Blum, Ivor Bowen, Simon Holmes, Raia Faith Baster, Lisa Jackson, Annshar Wolfs, Jason Shorter, Britt Hollingworth, Tiana Hokins, Becky Aizen, Bruce Thurlow, Alana Napurrula, Tricia Meeley, Jill Berry, Trent Headlam, Deborah Kelly, Adam Krongold, Diego Bonetto, Belinda Raposo, Cecile Knight, Tim Woods, Tia Crane, Jeremy Fullerton, Tracy Anthony, Sandy Lee Jones, Vivienne and Ross Ulman, Su Dennett, David Holmgren, James Stuart, Nicola Hensel, Zara Pearson, Franziska and John Ielo, Kathryn Pegiel, Angharad Wynne-Jones, Greg Foyster, Stuart and Tammi Jonas, Candice Boyd, Robert and Jan Jones, Petrus Spronk, Sam and Jackie Jones, Mariana Teuila Isara, Lena Mazza, Geoffrey and Georgina Williams, Jeff Brownscombe, Rakaia Nault, Henrietta and Ant Cheshire, Kate Gerritsen, Luke Pither, Lucas Ihlein, Louise Cruikshank, Michelle Carmela Fiordaliso, Geoffrey Michael Clark, Vanessa and Chris Wood, Matthew Phelan, Clay Ravin, Anne Gleeson, Angela Nikulinsky, Kath and Liam Wratten, اشر الاتيهم, Ant Petrucci, Fe Porter, Mel Ogden, Dora Berenyi, Kate Ulman, Bren Eisner, Abigail Ulman, Sophie Chishkovsky, Emily and D'Angelo Ulman, Trudy and Primo Clutterbok, Jacinta and Cameron Saunders, Laurel Freeland, Dallas Kinnear, Ian Robertson, Vivienne Thwaites, Gerry Bobsien, Denise Martin, Shane Herrington, John Sider, Megan

The Art of Free Travel

Spencer, Huw and Wendy Kingston, Kylie and Paul Smith, Jill Cockram, Kirsten Barnett Brown, Guy Brown, Kate Fagan, Peter Minter, Danielle and Mark Wheeler, Dave and Emily Berlach, Carol Marando, Jon Ellis, Deborah and Rod Lennon, Tom Dean, Fiona Anderson, Phil Smith, Michelle Gearin, Tom Kearney, Suzy Bates, Dom Jaskierniak, Chris Brown, Brian and Doris Corcoran, Glenn and Maryanne Handford, Brett Adamson, Kurt Adamson, Kevin and Lowanna Doye, Steve Henderson, Gull Herzberg, Adam Kornhauser, Kathy Ross, David Coyle, Steve Hill, Mark and Denise Feeney, Linda Marney, Rhoda Roberts, Eddy Carroll, Deanne Huckstepp, Sonia Romeyn, Phil Aitken, Natalia West, Bridget Kearny, Eka Eiff, Jessie Cole, Jan Cole, Kelly and Wendy Stack, Michelle and Luke Lennard, Linda Tait, Peppe and Jeanie Tucci, Rebecca Ryan, Mick and Jenny Harris, Tim Burder, Fiona Robson, Julie and Alistair Frame, Peter Skipworth, Saeng Mouykeng, Tim and Elaine McGreen, Duncan Murray, Dora Gibson, Clarry Bowen, Neville Bowen, Sarah Hoyal, Renée Lees, Simon Penrose, Gary and Jenny Trindall, Gary McClelland, Nick Ritar, Kirsten Bradley, Fiona Weir Walmsley, Adam Walmsley, Maarten Langeslag, Marlies Mulder, Peter O'Mara, Sam Dekok, Nick Sara, Larch Trumpetvine, Jeff Stewart, Cath Davies, Alison Wilken, Mel Pickering, Ronnie Ayliffe, Phil Norris, Meghan and Ian Campbell, Annie Werner, Genevieve Derwent, Alex Woodger, Robyn Rosenfeldt, Dale and Jenni from Merrimbula, Fraser Bailey, Kirsti Wilkinson, Jo Kidd, Tony Soccio, Chris Foster, Theresa Clancy, Dave Caudwell, Emma Ireland, Glen Dunn, Lindy Churches, Nicholas Hansen, Sally McCrae, Alberta Hornsby, Ashley Boyd, Jacquie Mackay, Lavina Mooner, Uncle Wally Stewart, Corey Stewart, Ben Grubb, Jim and Jeni Grubb, Jaala Freeman, Shannon Freeman, Yael Zalchendler, Matthew Newton Haines-powell, Maya Ward, John Reid, Tanya Loos, Chris Mclean, and all those chanced upon kind strangers and otherwise friends, both on the road and in the blogosphere. We thank Elspeth Menzies, Emily Stewart, Foong Ling Kong, and all at NewSouth Publishing for making this part of the ride so enjoyable. And we especially thank our boys – Zephyr, Blackwood and Zero – three-fifths of Artist as Family, for your spirit of adventure, togetherness and dissent.